BETTER DEAD

by Alan Ayckbourn

‖SAMUEL FRENCH‖

FOR AMATEUR PRODUCTION ENQUIRIES

UNITED KINGDOM AND WORLD
EXCLUDING NORTH AMERICA
licensing@concordtheatricals.co.uk
020-7054-7200

Each title is subject to availability from Concord Theatricals,
depending upon country of performance.

MUSIC USE NOTE

Licensees are solely responsible for obtaining formal written permission from copyright owners to use copyrighted music in the performance of this play and are strongly cautioned to do so. If no such permission is obtained by the licensee, then the licensee must use only original music that the licensee owns and controls. Licensees are solely responsible and liable for all music clearances and shall indemnify the copyright owners of the play(s) and their licensing agent, Concord Theatricals, against any costs, expenses, losses and liabilities arising from the use of music by licensees. Please contact the appropriate music licensing authority in your territory for the rights to any incidental music.

IMPORTANT BILLING AND CREDIT REQUIREMENTS

If you have obtained performance rights to this title, please refer to your licensing agreement for important billing and credit requirements.

BETTER OFF DEAD

First performed at the Stephen Joseph Theatre, Scarborough, in the Round auditorium on 11 September 2018, with the following cast:

ALGY WATERBRIDGE	Christopher Godwin
JESSICA WATERBRIDGE	Eileen Battye
THELMA BOSTOCK	Liz Jadav
JASON RATCLIFFE	Laurence Pears
GUS CREWES	Leigh Symonds
DCI TOMMY MIDDLEBRASS	Russell Dixon
DS GEMMA PRICE	Naomi Petersen

Director Alan Ayckbourn
Designer Michael Holt
Lighting Jason Taylor
Associate Sound Designer Paul Stear

CHARACTERS

ALGY WATERBRIDGE – an author, seventies
JESSICA WATERBRIDGE – his wife, seventies
THELMA BOSTOCK – his PA, fifties
JASON RATCLIFFE – his publisher, thirties
GUS CREWES – a journalist, seventies

The Figments
DCI TOMMY MIDDLEBRASS – fifties
DS GEMMA PRICE – mid-twenties

TIME

Over a week or so of one summer.

SETTING

The summerhouse and part of the surrounding garden of the Waterbridge's remote home in rural Yorkshire.

ACT I

Scene One

The summerhouse and part of the surrounding garden of the Waterbridge's remote home in rural Yorkshire.

The summerhouse itself is probably originally Victorian but has been recently modernised and converted into a writing workplace for Algy. Brick-built, hexagonal, with windows on the three sides facing south, with a single doorway at the back leading out, via a pathway, to the unseen house.

The garden is a "wild garden," favouring shrubs, trees, low bushes and wildflowers rather than a formal layout. Vegetation has been encouraged to run wild, with an occasional bright splash of colour against a background of varying greens. The paths that weave maze-like, hither and thither, are made of loose gravel rather than formal paving.

At the far end of the garden is the (also unseen) boundary wall which leads, by way of a gate, to the country lane beyond. At this end of the garden there is also a weathered wooden bench.

All in all, it is the most perfect, secluded and private space.

At the start, the area is in semi-darkness, lit only by a watery moon, and it is apparently the middle of the night. An owl hoots.

After a moment, from the far end of the garden, the bulky figure of **DCI TOMMY MIDDLEBRASS** *enters stealthily. He is a craggy Yorkshire detective who has seen and experienced just about everything there is to experience.*

He is followed by the slimmer figure of his long-suffering loyal sidekick, **DS GEMMA PRICE,** *somewhat less experienced than her DCI, but learning fast.*

TOMMY *(softly, rather impatiently)* Come on, Sergeant, don't hang about, woman!

GEMMA *(softly, nervously)* I don't think we should be doing this, guv, I honestly don't –

TOMMY Oh, for God's sake, you great whingeing hunk of angel cake –

GEMMA How do we know this bloke's even here?

TOMMY Trust me, he's here all right. Or hereabouts. I can tell it in me water. It's a well-known saying, lass, DCI Tommy Middlebrass's water's never far wrong.

GEMMA With respect, guv, we need a lot more justification than your bladder before we start breaking and entering, surely? We need a warrant, don't we? If we enter without a warrant, it'll constitute illegal trespass –

TOMMY Bugger all that! We don't need a warrant, lass, not to reconnoitre. This is just reconnoitre. In the old days, what we used to call a casual spontaneous reconnoitre. Perfectly legal.

GEMMA These days known as illegal search –

TOMMY Perhaps that's what you called it back in Sussex. That's not what we call it up here, love –

GEMMA *(wearily)* Surrey. For the hundredth time, Surrey –

TOMMY – I would remind you you're in Yorkshire now, lass –

GEMMA – I don't need reminding –

TOMMY – And up here, we do things different!

GEMMA You're telling me!

TOMMY Listen, people like this bloke in there, people like Leonard Arthur Hemp, if they deliberately choose to put themselves outside the law, disregard it when it suits them, like, they can't suddenly turn round and demand their legal rights, can they? Fair dos. They can't have it both ways, can they? They've broken the contract. They're no longer covered. They're out of benefit. Their legal cover's expired. They get what's coming, serve 'em bloody right. Now, you up for this or not, you southern softie?

GEMMA *(shaking her head, muttering)* The things you call me, I don't know why I put up with it...

TOMMY Cos I'm a brilliant copper, lass, that's why. Now, follow on. And mind how you go. It's dark along here so watch your feet, girl. We don't want you toppling over a garden gnome...

They grope their way forward cautiously.

At this point, the light gradually begins to build on **ALGY WATERBRIDGE** *in the summerhouse, seated typing at his keyboard.*

GEMMA *(as they go)* Should have brought the torch, shouldn't we? Left it in the car.

TOMMY Don't need a torch. Wake the bugger up, else, won't we?

GEMMA Assuming he's even home.

They move a little further.

What's it you've got against this bloke? It's really personal this, isn't it?

TOMMY Aye, very personal. Remind me to tell you about it sometime. The complete history of me and Leonard Arthur Hemp. He's highly dangerous this one –

GEMMA *(stubbing her toe on something)* Ow!

TOMMY – You right? – He's killed before and he won't hesitate to kill again. Ten years since he last struck, but he'll still have the taste. They never quite lose it. The taste for blood.

GEMMA If he's that dangerous, what are we doing in his back garden in the middle of the night with no backup?

TOMMY Just going to take a look in the window, that's all. Get the lie of the land, like. I said, this is just a casual reconnoitre. We just happened to be passing, we heard something odd, not quite right, untoward, like. And you said to me, "Hello, did you hear that, guv –?"

GEMMA Did I?

TOMMY – And I said, "Yes, Sergeant, I certainly did. I think we should investigate without delay, don't you? There may, after all, be human life at stake."

GEMMA Honestly, guv, brilliant copper or not, there are times when you don't half talk a load of – *(bumping into something)* Ow! Shit!

TOMMY You right?

GEMMA You weren't joking about garden gnomes, were you –

TOMMY *(disappearing off)* Wait there! Won't be a moment!

GEMMA *(left alone, to herself)* I think I've broken my sodding toe...

She sits on the bench, nursing her foot, as ALGY *continues with the narration. At this point, the convention is established that, whenever he narrates, he speaks directly into the dictation system built into his laptop. Whereas during the Middlebrass dialogue sections, his hands move silently over the keyboard.*

GEMMA, *during the next, limps off after* TOMMY, *colliding with further obstacles and silently cursing as she does so.*

ALGY *(speaking into his laptop mic)* ...Despite his not inconsiderable girth, Gemma concluded that Tommy Middlebrass must possess the night vision of a cat, so swiftly and effortlessly did he move along the winding paths, skilfully avoiding all unseen obstacles, the self-same obstacles which the luckless sergeant found herself drawn to as if by some invisible magnet. The watery excuse for a moon which had afforded them, till now, some faint illumination finally conceded defeat and retreated behind thick cloud. The darkness had now become impenetr–

JESSICA WATERBRIDGE enters from the house, abruptly interrupting ALGY in mid-flow.

The lighting changes sharply and the garden is flooded with morning sunshine. Birds sing.

JESSICA *(calling loudly and cheerfully)* I'm just popping down to the shops –

ALGY *(startled by the interruption)* Wah! *(angrily, to the screen)* Stop dictation!

JESSICA – Won't be long! Back in a tick!

She turns and goes out again as suddenly as she arrived.

ALGY *(vainly, after her)* How many more times do I have to tell you not to interrupt me when I'm working? How often do I have to say it? *(rising, shouting angrily at no one in particular)* How the hell can I possibly create a masterpiece when I'm continually being interrupted?

He takes an angry turn around the garden to work off his fury. Finally calming down, he returns to his seat, takes a deep breath and prepares to resume writing.

(gathering his thoughts) Where was I? *(after a pause, frustrated)* I've forgotten where I'd got to now. Bloody hell! *(studying the screen)* Where did I get to? *(re-reading his*

last sentence) "The darkness had now become – I'm just popping down to the shops –" Oh, for Christ's sake!

He angrily stabs the backspace key several times. The lights, during the next, dim back to their previous nighttime state.

(muttering as he does so) I'm just popping down to the sodding shops! Now then. *(bracing himself to continue)* After a moment, satisfied the house was unoccupied, they returned to the garden.

TOMMY *and* **GEMMA** *return.*

TOMMY Place is deserted.

GEMMA Said it would be.

TOMMY All right, clever dick.

GEMMA There's still no positive evidence he's even back in the district, is there?

TOMMY He's here. I can tell...

GEMMA – Yes, I know, you told me, it's in your water...

TOMMY No, I can smell he's here. I can smell the bugger. It's in my nose. He's here, I know he is. Ready and waiting for another victim.

GEMMA What with your water and your nose, I don't know why we bother with a crime kit. CSI's redundant, isn't it?

TOMMY Bugger CSI! I'd trust my nose sooner than that lot. Come on then, Sussex smart arse, time for a pint. You fancy one, do you?

He heads back across the garden.

GEMMA *(following him)* I keep saying, I can't drink that stuff...

TOMMY Yorkshire ale, lass! Best in the world! How I ever got landed with you, I'll never know...

GEMMA If it's any consolation, the feeling's mutual, guv...

They leave.

ALGY Once back in the village, Middlebrass wasted no time and made straight for the public bar, leaving the reluctant Gemma to park the car, as she did so, preparing herself for another long evening ahead. For she knew to her cost, Tommy was never a man to quit a pub before last orders or frequently long after into the small hours. Gemma sighed to herself. There was, after all, only so long she could spend eking out one small glass of pink tonic...

Under this last, **THELMA BOSTOCK** *has made her way cautiously from the house and now stands behind* **ALGY.**

THELMA *(softly, under him)* Algy... Algy... *(slightly louder)* Algy!

The lights abruptly resume their daylight state.

ALGY *(loudly and savagely)* WHAT? WHAT THE HELL IS IT NOW, FOR GOD'S SAKE? *(belatedly, to the screen)* End dictation!

THELMA *(jumping nervously)* Algy, you haven't forgotten your meeting this morning, have you?

ALGY Meeting? What meeting?

THELMA With this journalist.

ALGY What bloody journalist?

THELMA You agreed to meet him this morning.

ALGY I'm not meeting anyone this morning. Especially not a journalist.

THELMA But you agreed to this meeting, Algy, you really did. You said at the time you were perfectly happy to do it. It's been in your diary for weeks.

ALGY I never look in my diary, you know that.

THELMA That's hardly my fault, is it? You agreed to meet him today and I put it in your diary specially, so you wouldn't forget.

ALGY Well, I had. I'd entirely forgotten.

THELMA He's an old school friend, apparently. You agreed to see him.

ALGY What's his name?

THELMA *(consulting a slip of paper in her hand)* Gus Crewes.

ALGY Gus Crewes?

THELMA C – R – E – W – E – S. Crewes. He was at school with you, apparently.

ALGY Gus Crewes? I was never at school with anyone called Gus Crewes.

THELMA It seems he was a year or two below you. I did mention this over a month ago, Algy. You said you vaguely remembered him and were perfectly happy to talk to him.

ALGY Gus Crewes? *(shaking his head)* No. Don't remember him at all. Below me, you say? Probably fagged for me. Made my bed. Fetched and carried. Tidied my study, that sort of thing.

THELMA *(dryly)* Much like we do now, then?

ALGY What are you talking about? I've never asked you to make my bed.

THELMA No, Mrs. Henshaw does that, doesn't she? I do practically everything else, though.

ALGY Nonsense. You never have to clean the house or do the washing? Or the cooking?

THELMA – No, that's Mrs. Henshaw, as well.

ALGY Then, what are you talking about? You do bugger all. Living a life of luxury, I don't know what I pay you for.

THELMA All I'm saying, Algy, is you never have to do anything for yourself. Practically nothing. Apart from writing, that is –

ALGY Apart from writing? What do you mean, *apart* from writing –?

THELMA – Yet the moment I ask you to do a simple thing like look in your diary –

At this point (and it won't by any means be the last occasion it occurs) ALGY *lapses into what can best be described as "Middlebrass-speak." His accent becomes northern and his vocabulary noticeably coarsens. It's as if his darker ID had suddenly emerged.*

ALGY *(indignantly)* What the bloody hell are you talking about? I don't do anything? I would remind you, lass, you're talking to a major fucking novelist – so watch yourself –

THELMA Yes, well, I just wish that, as a major novelist, you would –

ALGY I sit out here out the back in this – shack, slaving away! Rain or shine. Sleet or snow. Just so that you lot can be fed and clothed, have a sodding roof over your heads. I'd remind you that, but for my creative genius, you'd all be out on the bloody streets! Earning a living the hard way. It's thanks to me you're living in the lap of luxury, I would remind you. If I didn't churn out sentence after sodding sentence, year in, year out –

THELMA *(over this last)* – Yes, all right, Algy, all right –

ALGY – Paragraph after pissing paragraph –

THELMA – Algy, that will do!

ALGY – Book after buggering book –

THELMA *(finally silencing him)* ALGY! THAT'S ENOUGH!

A silence.

ALGY *(finally, truculently)* Well. *(muttering)* Count yourself lucky you don't find yourself back on traffic, that's all.

THELMA Traffic?

ALGY Nothing.

THELMA Back on traffic? What on earth are you talking about?

ALGY You know what I mean.

THELMA God, that man, honestly. He's taken over again, hasn't he?

ALGY What man?

THELMA Tommy Middlebrass. I can tell you're writing him. I can always tell. He takes you over. The minute you start a new book. You get as bad as him, don't you?

ALGY How do you mean?

THELMA A self-opinionated bully. I'm not your detective sergeant, you know. Poor woman, I don't know how she puts up with it, I really don't.

ALGY She loves it. Secretly.

THELMA I very much doubt that.

ALGY Got a thing for him. Only she won't admit it. She does. Come on. So do you, if you're honest. You've got a bit of a thing for Tommy, as well, haven't you?

THELMA *(evasively, a trifle flustered)* All I'm saying – and I know, I know, I'm aware that I am talking to one of our major living writers, I hadn't forgotten – all I'm saying, Algy, is the world also consists of people other than yourself and your fictional characters, brilliant as they may be. And I do wish occasionally you would consider the rest of us in the real world. That's all I'm saying.

A slight pause. **ALGY** *glares at his screen.*

How's it going? Are you making progress?

ALGY *(muted, depressed)* Comes and goes. Fits and starts. I don't know.

THELMA Look, are you prepared to see this man or not? Otherwise I'll send him away. But he has come all the way from East Sussex.

ALGY East Sussex? Why the hell's he coming from East Sussex?

THELMA He lives there. He's freelance, apparently.

ALGY Freelance?

THELMA So he says.

ALGY God! He's not from *The Mail on Sunday*, is he?

THELMA I don't imagine *The Mail on Sunday* would be particularly interested in you, surely? Not unless you've done something dreadful.

ALGY Like murdering my staff?

THELMA Look, as soon as you've seen him, you get a really good run at it. I know all these interruptions must be so frustrating, I do understand. But once you've finished with this man, the next few days you've got absolutely nothing at all in the diary. It's completely clear. Days and days of uninterrupted writing time.

ALGY *nods glumly. He rocks to and fro, deciding.*

THELMA *waits.*

ALGY (*finally, grudgingly*) Well. I can give him five minutes. I can't stop work longer than that. I'll lose the flow. I'm poised here in mid-chapter.

THELMA I'll tell him he can only have a few moments.

ALGY When's he due?

THELMA (*glancing at her watch*) Any minute now, actually.

ALGY Now?

THELMA We arranged to make it eleven. Give you time to get out of bed.

ALGY (*stiffly*) I have been working out here since the crack of dawn, I'll have you know.

JESSICA *enters from the house as before.*

JESSICA (*calling loudly and cheerfully*) I'm just popping down to the shops –

ALGY *stares at her.*

THELMA *(equally cheerfully)* Righty-ho, Jessica, see you later!

JESSICA – Won't be long! Back in a tick!

She turns and goes out again.

A slight pause.

ALGY *and* **THELMA** *watch her go.*

ALGY She's getting worse, isn't she?

THELMA *(concerned)* Yes.

ALGY She's already said that to me once this morning. Only minutes ago.

THELMA Yes, she's said it to me, too. Several times.

ALGY Worrying.

THELMA It would be really worrying if she did try and go to the shops on her own. God knows if she'd ever find her way there. And as for getting back again...

ALGY That bad, is it?

THELMA Don't worry, I'll walk down with her later, once I've seen this man in. I've got one or two bits and bobs to update, too, on the website.

ALGY My website?

THELMA Of course yours. I don't have one, do I? I try and keep it up-to-date, you know. I don't totally fritter away my days, even if you think I do.

ALGY *(gloomily)* Don't know why you bother. There can't be much to update, these days, surely?

THELMA You'd be surprised. There's always something. Some new translation, usually Eastern European...

ALGY Oh, good-o. All of ten p, then. That'll pay the rent.

THELMA And that television company from Finland, they're still in touch occasionally, about making a new version of Middlebrass, did I tell you?

ALGY In Finnish?

THELMA Presumably.

ALGY Good luck to them.

THELMA Now, you mustn't be defeatist, Algy. You'll be back in fashion soon. Things come full circle, eventually. All the best writers go out of fashion, now and then. Till they're rediscovered.

ALGY *(dryly)* Can't wait.

A slight pause.

(impatiently) Where the hell is this bastard, then?

THELMA It's only just gone eleven.

ALGY Well, he's late. He is now eating into valuable writing time.

THELMA He'll be here soon

ALGY Just as I was on a roll.

THELMA Oh, dear. Poor you.

A slight pause.

I'm afraid, my mother's going much the same way as Jessica, you know. She gets up to go to the bathroom in the middle of the night and then she...

ALGY Ah, and then she can't find it?

THELMA Oh, yes, she can find her way there, all right. Mercifully. But after she's – been, she often can't find her way back again. I found her one night in the box room searching frantically for her bed. Claiming someone had stolen it.

ALGY Oh, dear.

THELMA You haven't had that sort of problem with Jessica yet, have you?

ALGY Not yet. That's something to look forward to.

(dryly) Can't wait for that.

A doorbell jangles in the distance.

THELMA Ah, here he is. Ready for him, are you?

ALGY As I'll ever be.

THELMA Now. Don't forget to mention the new book, will you?

ALGY The one I'm struggling here to finish, you mean? The one he is now actively stopping me from finishing...?

THELMA *(admonishingly)* Algy...

ALGY All right, all right, I'll remember. I wish to hell I could remember him, that's all.

THELMA *(as she leaves)* Maybe once you see his face, it'll come flooding back. Gus Crewes. Remember... Gus – Crewes...

She leaves.

After a moment, **ALGY,** *frowning, closes his laptop.*

ALGY Gus Crewes? Gus Crewes...? *(shaking his head)* No. Don't remember him from Adam.

He paces up and down, going through a little private ritual in the manner of someone unused to meeting strangers, in an effortful attempt to gear himself up into a sunnier persona, forcing his face into a ghastly smile.

(as he paces) Ha – ha! Ha – ha – ha! Well, well, well, well, well! Aha! Ha – ha! *(tiring from the effort, wearily)* God! How I loathe strangers!

THELMA *returns with* **GUS CREWES,** *a careworn, rather neglected, unloved-looking man.*

THELMA This way, just out here!

GUS Hello, there.

ALGY *(somewhat over-effusively)* My God! Gus Crewes! By all that's holy! My dear fellow! My word, my word! How good to see you after all this time, old chap.

GUS *(a little taken aback)* Algy! You remember me?

ALGY How could I forget old Gus Crewes?

GUS It's been quite a few years. I thought you might have done.

THELMA *(loyally)* Algy never forgets a face. He's remarkable like that.

GUS It's been rather a long time. I was somewhat junior to you, of course...

ALGY *(indicating the summerhouse)* Do come in, dear chap, have a seat.

GUS Thank you.

THELMA I was going to offer Mr. Crewes a cup of coffee...

GUS Oh, lovely, if it's not too much trouble...

THELMA Not at all. Would you like coffee as well, Algy?

ALGY No, thanks, not just at the moment.

GUS *(immediately retracting)* Ah, well, in that case, I don't think I will either...

THELMA It's no trouble, really...

GUS No, really. No, thank you...

THELMA Really? You're quite sure? I was just on the point of making some...?

GUS No, no, really, please...

THELMA You're quite sure?

GUS Really and truly.

THELMA *(after a slight pause)* Well, I'll leave you both to it, then.

ALGY I wouldn't say no to a glass of water, Thelma. If you're passing a tap.

THELMA Yes, of course. Would you care for a glass of water, Mr. Crewes?

GUS Lovely, thank you. If it's not too much trouble...

THELMA Not at all.

GUS Thank you.

THELMA You're sure you won't change your mind and have a coffee...?

GUS No, no, no...

THELMA You're perfectly certain? It's really no –

ALGY *(sharply)* Thelma, just bring him a glass of water, for God's sake!

> THELMA *goes off.* GUS *looks nervous. A pause.*

GUS *(looking around)* So this is where it all happens, eh?

ALGY Sorry?

GUS *(producing a small recording device)* Sorry. You don't object to these things, do you?

ALGY No, not at all. Best to get these things accurate.

GUS *(laughing)* A lot safer than my rusty shorthand, anyway.

> *He sets up his recorder.*

> Yes, as I say, I was a year or two junior to you. I'm amazed you even remembered me...

ALGY If I recall correctly, didn't you used to fag for me, at one stage?

GUS What a memory! Yes, I did. I used to clean your wicket-keeping pads.

ALGY Aha!

> *A slight pause.*

> My wicket-keeping pads?

GUS Yes, rather badly, if I recall. Wet white all over the straps...

He laughs.

ALGY I never had any wicket-keeping pads.

GUS You didn't?

ALGY I never kept wicket.

GUS No?

ALGY I loathed cricket.

GUS Did you?

ALGY Never played if I could possibly avoid it. I was strictly a squash man. I used to play a lot of squash.

GUS Ah!

ALGY Perhaps you used to polish my racket?

GUS *(slightly mystified)* No, I can't remember doing that –

ALGY Or possibly scrubbed my squash balls, eh?

He laughs.

GUS *(laughing nervously)* No, no, I'm sure I would have remembered doing that –

ALGY *(laughing)* Yes, I'm sure you would have done.

They laugh again.

Quite a bit of that in our day, wasn't there?

GUS Yes. Oh, Lord, yes. *(hastily resuming his task)* One... Two... Three... Testing. Gus Crewes talking to Algy Waterstone.

He plays it back.

Yes, that all seems to be working...

ALGY Waterbridge.

GUS Sorry?

ALGY Water*bridge*. The name's Water*bridge*.

GUS *(blankly)* Water*bridge*?

ALGY Water*bridge*.

GUS Water*bridge*? You prefer that emphasis, do you?

ALGY What?

GUS You prefer the emphasis on the second syllable? On the bridge? Water*bridge*?

ALGY No. Just plain Waterbridge.

GUS *(thoroughly confused)* Ah!

ALGY Only you said Water*stone*. My name's not Waterstone, it's Waterbridge.

GUS Oh, I see. Did I say Waterstone? I meant to say Waterbridge. I do beg your pardon.

He laughs.

ALGY Best to get the name correct. Start off on the right foot, anyway.

He laughs.

GUS *(laughing)* Waterstone! What on earth was I thinking of? Waterstone! Probably thinking of the pub, wasn't I?

ALGY *(slightly mystified)* The pub?

GUS Waterstones.

ALGY I think you're thinking of Wetherspoon's.

GUS Wetherspoon's! Yes of course! I don't know why I said Waterstones. Wetherspoon's. I meant Wetherspoon. Algy Wetherspoon, of course. Sorry.

ALGY Waterbridge.

GUS Sorry?

ALGY Waterbridge. Algy Waterbridge. Not Wetherspoon.

GUS Waterbridge, yes. Sorry.

He laughs.

A slight pause.

ALGY You do a lot of this sort of thing, do you?

GUS Sorry?

ALGY In-depth interviews? You do a lot of them, do you?

GUS Well, actually, I tend to specialise in obituaries. Of late.

ALGY Obituaries?

GUS Most of the people I write about are usually dead and gone by the time I get to them. To be perfectly frank, I'm finding it a bit off-putting, talking to someone who's still alive and kicking.

He laughs.

ALGY *(laughing)* Ah, well, at least the dead can't complain if you get their name wrong, can they?

GUS *(laughing)* No...no...

ALGY Mind you, you might just get a bit of flack from the relatives.

He laughs.

GUS *(laughing)* Yes...yes...

ALGY But I'm afraid, in my case, you're a trifle early. I'm not dead yet.

GUS *(laughing)* Oh, dear, that's too bad. *(realising his gaffe)* For me, that is. Too bad for me.

A slight pause.

Sorry.

THELMA *returns with two glasses of water on a tray.*

THELMA Sorry to take so long.

GUS Thank you so much. That's really most kind of you.

THELMA Not at all, you're very welcome. And you're sure you won't change your mind and have a cup of coff–

ALGY *(sharply)* He's perfectly happy with water, Thelma.

GUS Perfectly.

THELMA Just call out if you need anything, won't you? Biscuits, tea, coffee? I think there's even a little bit of seed cake left over from the other day, Algy...

GUS looks eager and about to say yes. ALGY's look says otherwise.

No? Right.

She leaves.

GUS That's what we could all do with, eh, the love of a good woman?

ALGY Oh, yes...

GUS What every chap could do with, eh?

ALGY Rather...

GUS A good wife behind him, eh?

ALGY She's not my wife.

GUS She isn't?

ALGY She's my secretary.

GUS Secretary?

ALGY Secretary. PA. General dogsbody. Perfectly pleasant but I wouldn't want to marry her.

GUS Oh, I understood she was your wife. I'm so sorry.

He shakes his head.

ALGY You have come to the right house, I take it?

GUS Yes, yes, sorry. I'm so sorry. I can't imagine what you must think of me.

He laughs.

ALGY *(unsmiling)* No. I'm sure you can't.

GUS *laughs again.*

A pause.

ALGY *stares at him.*

GUS *(in an attempt to restart things, brightly)* So. This is where it all happens, is it? The engine room? This is where it's all *at*, eh?

ALGY *(coolly)* This is where I write, yes. Mostly. When it's not either pissing down or freezing over. Which it tends to do ten months of the year, round these parts.

GUS Pleasant enough today, anyway.

ALGY Oh, yes. Nice enough today.

GUS I must say I envy you. Having somewhere away like this, away from it all, somewhere just to sit and write. In solitude. I envy you this. I don't have anywhere, you know. Nowhere.

ALGY No?

GUS I tend to do most of my writing, such as it is, in my bedroom. Only room in the house that's warm enough. Me, my fan heater and my trusty laptop. For twelve months of the year. In the cold and dark.

ALGY Twelve months of the year? My God! Where the hell do you live? Reykjavík?

GUS Eastbourne.

ALGY Ah.

GUS Private hotel. Seen better days, I'm afraid.

ALGY I see.

GUS Well, more of an old-fashioned boarding house really. Run by the very splendid Mrs. Jenkins. Who is the one redeeming blessing in my life. Peggy Jenkins. My saviour. Quite the most wonderful woman. Salt of the earth. Seen me through some – difficult times in my life, I can tell you. Diabolical times. Nightmare times. You know the phrase "to hell and back"? Well, I've been there, Algy, I can tell you, I've been there.

ALGY I'm sorry to hear that.

GUS To hell. And back. On a third-class return ticket, travelling steerage all the way. I can honestly say, Algy, without Peggy Jenkins, I'd probably have ended it all ages ago, you know. I'd never have got through it alone. There've been times, I don't mind telling you, when it all got – almost overwhelming. Like every breath was being sucked from my body.

ALGY Nasty feeling.

GUS I think if I'd had somewhere like this, at the start, my life would have taken a very different turn, I can tell you. If I'd had all this – *(waving his arm)* – I often look back and I think, if only things could have been different...different from...how...it all...yes. *(reflecting)* Still. Luck of the draw, eh? You happened to get lucky, that's all. Another day, another time, it could have been me, eh?

A slight pause.

ALGY Look, I'm terribly sorry to hear all this, old boy, I really am. It sounds like you – you've been through some harsh times, one way or another. And I do sympathise, I really do, but...

GUS Thank you, Algy, I knew you'd understand...

ALGY Yes, I do, I do, I really do, old chap, and I'd love to hear more, believe me. But I am midway through this confounded book and I was under the impression, don't get me wrong, but I was under the impression that you were here to interview me...

GUS *(guiltily)* Oh, God, yes, I'm so sorry...

ALGY ...I mean, I may have got entirely the wrong end of the stick...?

GUS No, no. It's me, Algy, it's entirely me. Sitting here talking about myself, typical. I'm always doing that. Typical. Some days, I come home from a major interview – Helen Mirren, say, or George – whateverhisnameis – whoever – and I switch on that recorder to play it back, to transcribe it and there it is, hour upon hour of me, droning on about myself. That's the worst thing about being a journalist, you know. Constantly having to listen to other people talking about themselves. Day in, day out. Listening endlessly to them droning on and on. Boasting about what they've done, what they hope to do, their dreams for the future. Boasting about their wretched spoilt kids. When all the time there's this voice at the back of my head shouting, "Oh, do shut up, just shut up for one minute! Why can't we talk about *me* for a change? Me, me, me?"

ALGY Yes, I take your point. I can see that's frustrating. But don't you feel, somewhere along the line, old boy, you may have made a wrong career choice?

JESSICA *enters from the house as before.*

JESSICA *(calling loudly and cheerfully)* I'm just popping down to the shops –

ALGY *(under his breath)* Oh, dear God!

GUS *(half rising)* Hello there. I don't think we've met, I'm –

JESSICA *(to GUS)* Oh, hello. Back to look at them again, are you?

GUS Sorry?

JESSICA They've become particularly smelly at this time of year –

GUS *(mystified)* Oh, yes? That must be a problem.

JESSICA I think it's this warm weather. Won't be long! Back in a tick!

She turns and goes out again.

GUS *(somewhat nonplussed)* Yes. Was that your –?

ALGY That was my wife. Jessica. I think she mistook you for someone else.

GUS Yes.

ALGY We've been having problems with the drains of late.

GUS Oh, I see.

ALGY She obviously mistook you for the drainage engineer we had in the other day. An easy mistake to make...

GUS Ah, yes.

ALGY Perhaps you should try that instead? If you decide to give up journalism? Drainage engineer?

GUS *laughs nervously, unsure if* ALGY*'s joking.*

Look, wrenching the subject back to me, if we could, in the few brief moments we have left...

GUS You know, I think you may have hit things on the head, Algy.

ALGY What?

GUS What you said about me making the wrong career choice, I think you may have nailed it, old boy. You see, I never had the choice. Soon as I left school, it was journalism or nothing. My father was editor of the local rag, my mother was a features writer. It was in the blood, you see. It was always journalism or nothing in our family. Ever since I can remember. Goes back generations. From the local rag, I went straight to *The Mail on Sunday.*

ALGY Oh, did you now?

GUS Only there a couple of months, couldn't settle. Wrong crowd, as far as I was concerned. Far too many strong-minded, self-opinionated women, for my taste. So then a stint on the *Express*, a month or two on *The News of the World* until it sadly folded. Since then, footloose, freelance and fancy-free. No editorial control. None at all. No semi-literate, sixteen-year-old subs breathing down your neck, nitpicking, tinkering with your copy. None of that. This way, I get the idea, I write it, I toss it in the air, first person to grab it... Perfect freedom.

ALGY You have someone in mind for this, I take it? Any potential grabbers for this one?

GUS *(cagily)* Let's just say, there are one or two interested parties. Highly interested. Enough said? I'm quite excited. Could come down to the wire.

ALGY Highest bidder, eh?

GUS You bet.

A silence. They both stare at the recording device sitting between them.

ALGY *(at length)* That thing still working, is it?

GUS *(grabbing hold of it, alarmed)* Oh, Lord.

He fiddles with the buttons, rewinds and presses play. His voice is heard from the device: "...Wrong crowd so far as I was concerned. Far too many strong-minded, self-opinionated women, for my –"

No, it's working fine. Relief.

ALGY *(dryly)* Just so long as it's picking you up, that's the main thing.

GUS God, yes! Must get on. Sorry.

ALGY Don't want to miss the late editions, do we?

GUS Lord, no, thing of the past. None of that. All digital these days, of course. Everything's effing digital. E-books. Kindles. Tweets and blogs and twitters. Rare to get your hands on a good solid piece of paper these days, isn't it? Feel it between your fingers. Get to smell it. God, the smell of it! Remember? Did you used to sniff books when you were a kid? I did.

I used to lie in bed every Christmas morning, sniffing my new *Rupert Annual*. Sheer heaven! God, what joy that was! Those were the days, eh?

ALGY Talking of books, I'm just in the middle of a new one myself, as a matter of fact. In case you're interested...

GUS Oh, are you, are you, now?

ALGY ...Which you're most welcome to have a sniff at, once it's published. When it's published. If it's published.

GUS How exciting. A brand-new one, then?

ALGY Well. Another in the series, you know.

GUS Oh, great! Another *Silly Milly*, that's great news!

ALGY Another what?

GUS You know, *Silly Milly*.

ALGY *(incredulously)* *Silly Milly*?

GUS *Silly Milly and Horrid Horace*, you know.

ALGY *Silly Milly and Horrid Horace*? Where the hell did you get those from?

GUS You did write those, didn't you? God, I haven't got that wrong as well, have I? I've got the right author? You did write the *Milly and Horace* books?

ALGY Yes. Years ago. Aeons ago. When my daughter was a kid. When she had – Sarah had nocturnal problems. We used to read her to sleep with them.

GUS Oh, that's a charming story. You used to read them to her personally, did you?

ALGY No, Jessica did mostly. But they were never published. Never seen the light of day. They're still stuck in a drawer somewhere, if they haven't been chucked out. They were purely for family. Private. Just between us. How the hell did you hear about them?

GUS I've read them.

ALGY Read them?

GUS A number of them, anyway. Online. I read them online.

ALGY Online? What the hell are they doing online?

GUS They're on your website.

ALGY My website?

GUS I went on your website when I was researching this interview –

ALGY Getting the name right and so on?

GUS – And I came across them. They're terrific stories. I really enjoyed them. Enormous fun. In my view, the best thing since Christopher Robin. Made me laugh out loud. Which is pretty rare for me.

He laughs.

ALGY Who the hell put them online, for Christ's sake?

GUS Didn't you?

ALGY I most certainly did not.

GUS Oh.

ALGY I have a good idea who did, though.

GUS So, what are you working on, if it isn't another *Silly Milly*?

ALGY My latest Middlebrass.

GUS Sorry, your latest what?

ALGY Middlebrass. Detective Chief Inspector Tommy Middlebrass of Grimthorpe CID. His latest case.

GUS Oh, him?

ALGY "Oh, him"? Have you ever read any?

GUS *(guardedly)* I – remember the TV series...

ALGY Do you?

GUS ...Vividly. Great television. For its time, of course. Huge viewing figures, too. I would imagine.

ALGY Vast.

GUS I mean, considering. Black-and-white, 405 lines and all that. Groundbreaking. For its day. Way ahead of its day. Very well acted.

ALGY You think so?

GUS Great theme tune, I seem to recall. *(trying unsuccessfully to remember it)* Doo – dee – doo! Dee-doooo – dee – dooo – deee...

ALGY I think you'll find that was *Z Cars*...

A silence. ALGY *looks grim. His Middlebrass ID looming dangerously close.*

GUS You didn't approve, I take it? Of the programmes?

ALGY I loathed every minute of them. Every excruciating second. Every single ghastly episode. It got progressively worse, series after series...

GUS Really? I didn't think it was that bad...

ALGY Have you read the books?

GUS *(who clearly hasn't)* Well...I've – dipped into them, you know...in places...

ALGY If you'd read any of the bloody books, you'd know the TV version was a complete travesty from start to finish – half the cast didn't even come from Yorkshire! *(in a bad mock Yorkshire accent)* "By hecky thump, lads, this is a fair rum do, sithee." That fat bitch who cast it deserved to be hung, drawn and quartered and stuck with a spike up her arse in the middle of Barnsley town centre.

GUS *(taken aback)* I thought the chap playing the main detective was excellent –

ALGY *(angrily)* He was a Welshman! She cast a fucking Welshman, for Christ's sake!

A silence.

GUS *is clearly shocked by the other's vehemence and change of persona...*

(in a low voice) I'll have you know, the Middlebrass books when they were first published, *The Times*' Literary Supplement described them as raising detective fiction to a new level on a par with Dickens, Conan Doyle or fucking Tolstoy. And they're not ones for mincing words, the TLS...

GUS *(impressed)* Good gracious, that's saying something...

ALGY My first novel. Seventeen years old, I was. Nobbut a lad. So, you can stick that in your bloody article, and all...

GUS Heavens! I had no idea.

ALGY *(regarding him with hostility)* No you don't, do you? No bloody idea at all, have you? Not a solitary sodding clue, have you?

GUS Well. I wouldn't go quite so far as that –

ALGY Wouldn't you? Well, I would, lad, I would. Fact, I'd go considerably further. You haven't got a fucking inkling! Yes, well I think that just about wraps it up, doesn't it? End of interview, don't you think? Interview terminated at eleven twenty-seven hours!

He picks up the recording device and abruptly switches it off.

GUS But I haven't quite finished my questions –

ALGY *(the full Middlebrass finally emerging)* Frankly, lad, you got no more questions to ask, have you? Considering you had trouble remembering my name, you clearly hadn't read a single serious word I've written and you muddled me up with the fucking school wicket-keeper! All in all, it's high time you buggered off back to Peggy Jenkins.

GUS Ah, no, come on be fair...

ALGY Have a good trip back, then.

GUS *(retreating)* Listen, Algy, I feel we may have got off on the wrong –

ALGY Excuse me, I have to get back to this novel that you're never likely to read.

GUS *(flustered)* Well, if you're quite sure...

ALGY *has turned his back on* GUS *and, reopening his laptop, prepares to resume writing.* GUS *hovers uncertainly in the doorway.*

(uncertainly) Sorry, if I've...yep... Right...

ALGY Have I not made myself clear, lad? *(loudly)* BUGGER OFF!

THELMA *enters, concerned, having heard this last.*

THELMA Anything the –? Oh! *(reading the situation, sotto to* GUS*)* Have you finished?

GUS *(still a bit bemused, sotto)* Yes, I think we... I think we... might have done...

THELMA *(sotto)* Got all you needed?

GUS *(sotto)* Oh, yes... I think so...just about...

THELMA *(sotto)* He can get a little moody. When he's writing. You mustn't take it personally. *(as they leave)* Are you going back by train?

GUS *(following her, sotto)* Yes, I'll walk back to the village and then catch the bus back into York...

THELMA *(sotto, as she goes)* You're sure you wouldn't care for a coffee before you go...?

They leave.

ALGY *(shaking his head)* Bloody unbelievable! Now then...

He shakes his head to clear it and, taking a deep breath, resumes his novel. The lights fade again to indicate nighttime.

(resuming) The saloon bar of The Angler's Rest was crowded with the usual local regulars, their numbers doubled by an influx of weekend holidaymakers. Gemma searched in vain for a free seat and had all but resigned herself to another evening propping up the bar when Tommy signalled to her to wait in the pub garden at the back.

GEMMA *enters and sits on the bench.*

It is now lit by the reflection of multicoloured ornamental bulbs in the pub garden. Pub sounds in the background.

Grateful to escape the crush and the din for the calm of the garden, she was happy to trade a reduction in temperature in return for fresh air and relative tranquillity.

TOMMY *enters, carrying a full pint and* GEMMA'*s pink tonic. A burst of sound from the pub behind him.*

TOMMY *(as he approaches)* ...There you go. One pink tonic. Presume that's what you wanted?

GEMMA Thanks.

TOMMY You never have a proper drink, then? You know, other than this? A real drink, like?

GEMMA Designated driver, aren't I? No choice. Glass of wine occasionally. Very occasionally.

TOMMY You don't smoke either?

GEMMA No, never.

TOMMY Never gamble?

GEMMA Don't see the point.

TOMMY Go to football? Cricket? Dog racing?

GEMMA *shakes her head to all these.*

Bloody hell, love. What the hell do you do for fun?

GEMMA *(smiling)* Never you mind.

TOMMY Hey, you're not off with Alfie Parks are you? Young Constable Parks?

GEMMA *smiles and shakes her head.*

Thought I caught him eyeing you up the other day. Reckon he fancies his chances there.

GEMMA In his dreams.

TOMMY No romance for you, then?

GEMMA Not at present.

TOMMY *(shaking his head, disapprovingly)* I don't know, you must be the first nun to join the police force...

GEMMA I enjoy the job, that's all. Don't want to get sidetracked.

TOMMY You need to get away, though. Take some downtime, you know. Everyone needs that occasionally.

GEMMA If I want downtime, I'll read a book.

TOMMY *(shaking his head, disgusted)* Incompatible, that's us. Incom – bloody – patible.

GEMMA *(smiling)* Make a good team, though, don't we?

TOMMY *(nodding)* Oh, aye. A good team. Give you that.

A slight pause.

GEMMA Well?

TOMMY What?

GEMMA You promised to tell me the complete story of you and Leonard Arthur Hemp. What you've got against him.

TOMMY So I did.

GEMMA What makes it so personal, then?

TOMMY Got an hour to spare, have you?

GEMMA If I'm risking my neck to nail him, I'd like a good reason.

TOMMY It's ancient history.

GEMMA We've got all night.

TOMMY Not without another drink I haven't.

GEMMA I'll get them. Same again?

TOMMY *(half rising)* No, it's all right, I'll –

GEMMA *(getting up)* No, it's my shout, guv. Wait there, I'll get them in. *(gathering up their glasses)* That's if you can bear to have a woman buying you a drink. I'm sure the ghost of your late dad would allow it, just this once.

TOMMY Doubt it. Not on a Friday. No women in pubs on Fridays, not in his day. Unwritten law.

GEMMA *(as she leaves)* Welcome back to the Stone Age.

TOMMY, *alone, stands thoughtfully.*

During the next, he wanders slowly the other way, out of sight.

ALGY As the sergeant went back inside, Tommy deliberated whether or not to tell Gemma the full story. Maybe past history, particularly that section of Grimthorpe's past history, was best left buried in the basement archive, filed under F for failed and fruitless. Deep in his own thoughts, Tommy wandered a little way and found himself staring at a deserted play area, provided by the management as a sop for their underage patrons. As he stared morosely at the swings, miniature roundabouts and rusting slides, he was sharply reminded of another playground, not a dozen miles from there, where he and DCI Gilpin had made that fateful, grisly discovery...

THELMA *enters. The lights resume their normal daytime state.*

THELMA *(as she returns)* ...Well, wasn't he a sweet man? Charming. I really took to him. He wasn't at all like most journalists, I think he was genuinely interested...

She tails off as she sees ALGY's *head has slumped on his keyboard in silent frustration at this interruption.*

ALGY *(muffled)* End dictation.

THELMA Oh, I'm sorry. Were you in mid-flow? I'm so sorry...

ALGY No, no, not at all. I was sitting here compiling nature notes for the local paper –

THELMA Well, I wasn't to know, was I –?

ALGY – This morning, I witnessed a cheeky altercation between a perky little sparrow and a quirky cuckoo –

THELMA – I mean, it's sometimes extremely difficult to tell when you're writing and when you're not writing, Algy, it really is –

ALGY – Both of them cheekily quarrelling as to who was to have first use of the birdbath –

THELMA – I mean, occasionally you sit there looking totally blank and you're actually writing –

ALGY – Tweet-tweet-tweet, cuckooo, cuckooo –

THELMA – And other times you're sitting there looking equally blank and it turns out you're not thinking of anything at all – *(huffily turning to leave)* I mean, you can't expect us to be mind readers, you know...

She starts to return to the house.

ALGY Hoy!

THELMA *(stopping)* What?

ALGY I want a word with you...

THELMA *(rather wearily)* What is it now?

ALGY *Milly and Horace...*

THELMA What?

ALGY *Silly Milly and Horrid Horace.* That halfwit was asking about them just now...

THELMA *(rather guiltily)* Oh, was he?

ALGY He wanted to know whether I was writing any more of them.

THELMA Oh, I do wish you would...

ALGY I asked him how he even knew about them. Since, as far as I'm aware, they've been locked away in a drawer in my study there. Haven't seen the light of day in forty years...

THELMA Such a shame.

ALGY Not only had he heard of them, he'd actually read them.

THELMA How odd.

ALGY On the Internet. On my website.

THELMA Right.

ALGY How the hell did they come to be on there in the first place, might I ask?

A slight pause.

THELMA I just thought they needed to be seen, that's all. I really did.

ALGY And you took it upon yourself to make a unilateral decision to publish them to the world, did you? Without a word to me?

THELMA I think they're utterly charming. Unusual. Original. And rather special.

ALGY They are also private documents. As I recall, handwritten in pencil, and solely intended to be read to my young daughter at bedtime. You had absolutely no business publishing them, without so much as a by your leave. I regard that as a total breach of employee confidence.

THELMA Oh, don't be so pompous, Algy. I felt they deserved to be read by a wider audience, that's all. So, I copied them out and then I posted them in a little subsection on their own, well away from anything else, under the separate heading, Odds and Bobs.

ALGY You had no business tampering with my website, entering unauthorised material, entirely off your own bat –

THELMA I'm the only one who ever does tamper with it, aren't I? You never even bother to look at it. I doubt if you've opened it in years –

ALGY You take that stuff off immediately, do you hear? That was private material which was specially written for my five-year-old daughter, God bless her –

THELMA – Whom you never see from one year to the next –

ALGY *(shouting)* Of course I don't! She's forty-six years old and living in Canada, for Christ's sake!

THELMA You could at least phone her – talk to her at least.

ALGY I loathe talking on the phone. You know that perfectly well.

THELMA She used to call in the old days. Regularly. She used to talk to Jessica every single week without fail. Until Jessica was – not able to talk to her anymore. Sarah used to write to you regularly, too, at one stage. But you were always far too busy to reply, of course. I think the poor girl gave up eventually.

ALGY We've nothing in common. Not a single thing. Her or her lumpen, big-boned Canadian brood. They're not interested in me, I don't give a damn about them. The only thing we have between us these days is 3,000 miles of polluted ocean.

THELMA *(shrugging)* At the rate you're going, Algy, I think you're probably going to die a very lonely man, you know.

She starts to go off.

ALGY At least I'll be better off, thankfully well out of it, thank God! *(yelling after her)* You take that stuff off my website, do you hear? At once!

THELMA *(returning briefly, coolly)* I will have you know that since I posted the *Milly and Horace* stories, it has had several hundred hits. Considerably more than your website has had in the previous ten years put together. So, somebody round here is doing something right, aren't they?

She goes off.

ALGY *(muttering)* Horrid Horace and Silly Milly. If that's all I'm to be remembered by, I'm better off dead, anyway, that's all I can say. *(gathering his thoughts)* Now, then...

He takes another deep breath and prepares to continue his writing. During the next, TOMMY wanders back, still deep in thought, to resume his previous position. The lights gradually dim to their nighttime state.

(re-reading) ...As Tommy stared morosely at the swings, miniature roundabouts and rusting slides, he was sharply reminded of another playground, not a dozen miles from there, where he and DCI Gilpin had made that fateful, grisly discovery...

He resumes typing.

GEMMA *re-enters with fresh drinks, a pint for TOMMY and another big tonic for her.*

The pub sounds resume as before.

GEMMA *(as she enters, calling)* ...Here you are. One pint of horrible brew...

TOMMY *(re-entering, still deep in his thoughts)* Ta.

GEMMA He's cheeky that barman, isn't he?

TOMMY What? Giving you lip, was he?

GEMMA God's gift to women, he reckons.

TOMMY He's harmless enough is Harry.

GEMMA He better be. Lucky for him I had my hands full.

TOMMY He's all talk, Harry. We go back a long way, me and
him. Cheers!

GEMMA Cheers! Got form then, has he?

TOMMY Couple of cases of minor GBH. You know, difficult
customers.

GEMMA I imagine he gets plenty of those, if his attitude to me
was anything to go by. *(sitting back on the bench)* Now, then.
Are you going to tell me about it? What you got against this
Hemp bloke that's so personal?

TOMMY Oh, aye. Him.

A slight pause.

Sure you want to hear?

GEMMA Bursting.

TOMMY It's not pleasant –

GEMMA I'm comfortable with unpleasant.

TOMMY Well. You heard tell of DCI Gilpin, I take it?

GEMMA I've heard, yes. Took early retirement, didn't he?

TOMMY Under pressure.

GEMMA Yes?

TOMMY From above, like, you know.

GEMMA Naughty boy, was he?

TOMMY What, Reg Gilpin? Straight as an arrow, Reg. Never
known a straighter copper. I was his DS for five years. Always
strictly by the rules. No, he were fitted up. Bastards fitted
him up.

GEMMA Who? Who fitted him up?

TOMMY Not who. What. Money. Money, love. Villains greasing the right palms at the right time. Heads turned away. Key evidence conveniently lost or gone missing. Reg never stood a chance. He shouldered the lot, fair and square. The full brunt himself. Shielded me from it entirely. Protected his bagman. Loyal to the end, him. Any road, ten years ago, one night in April, early evening, we got this shout from uniform. Something unusual in this garden, out at West Shale.

GEMMA What, the same one we were in this –?

TOMMY Aye, the same one we were just stood in. It were a posh area even in those days. Smart. Stockbrokers and that. Saucers with their cups. Any road, this householder next door, she'd spotted something peculiar, in the adjoining garden. Something not quite right. Called it in. By the time we both got there, Reg and me, we found this...this... *(hesitantly)* ...this lass... *(shakes his head at the memory)* ...fourteen years old... Her mother had sent her out in the garden to hang out the washing, you know... And – well – she weren't the brightest button in the box, you could say. But she didn't deserve... So she were hanging out the weekly wash, clothing and sheets and pillowcases and so on... And this fellow, he climbs over the fence and creeps up on the other side of the washing line. Behind the sheets, like, so she never sees him till the very last minute. And then he...he...

GEMMA Oh, God...

TOMMY He pulls one of the sheets over his head and pretends to be a ghost.

GEMMA *(surprised)* What?

ALGY *(equally surprised)* He did what?

TOMMY Frightened the poor lass half to death. As I say, she didn't have her complete set of marbles. Silly Milly Simpkins, she was known as, locally...

ALGY *(indignantly)* Just a minute! Just a minute! What the hell's going on here?

GEMMA I hope you caught the little bastard –?

TOMMY Aye, we caught him. Horace Hacksaw. Also known as Horrid Horace.

ALGY Oh, for God's sake! Stop this at once!

TOMMY We finally caught him –

GEMMA Glad to hear it –

TOMMY But not before he'd hidden her mother's clean knickers in the gooseberry bushes...

ALGY Right! That's enough!

GEMMA There's only one thing to do with that sort...

ALGY That's quite enough of that!

TOMMY Aye. Put 'em over your knee and wallop 'em...

GEMMA Send them to bed with no supper...

ALGY *(over this last, furiously drowning them out)* Shut up! Shut up! Shut up! SHUT UP! End dictation!

The lights are restored to daylight.

GEMMA *and* TOMMY *go off rapidly.*

ALGY *glares at his screen with fury.*

THELMA *enters from the house.*

What's going on here? What the hell's happening?

THELMA Algy!

ALGY *(unaware of her)* I'm going mad, I think I'm going mad! I must be going mad...

THELMA *(louder)* Algy! *(louder still)* ALGY!

ALGY *(glaring at her, savagely)* This is all your fault, you know!

THELMA Algy. Jessica's disappeared.

ALGY What?

THELMA She's gone walkabout. She's completely vanished. There's no sign of her anywhere.

ALGY *(more quietly)* What do you mean, vanished?

THELMA There's no sign of her anywhere.

ALGY *(staring at her, in a low voice)* This is a conspiracy, isn't it? You're all in it together, aren't you? All of you? I'm never going to finish this book, am I? That's your plan, isn't it? *(clasping the laptop to him protectively)* That's what you're all hoping for. Trying to stifle my creative genius –

THELMA *(sternly)* Algy! Will you pull yourself together! Jessica is missing! She is probably wandering somewhere, alone, lost and vulnerable. I would remind you that she is your wife, a living, breathing, flesh and blood human being. Whereas that – *(indicating the laptop)* – is only a wretched book!

ALGY *stares at her.*

Now, do come along and help me look for her, please.

She goes off.

(calling as she goes) Jessica! Jessica! Jessica!

ALGY *(stunned)* A wretched book? *Only* a book?

He shakes his head and puts down the laptop.

(with increasing incredulity) Only? *Only? ONLY A BOOK?* *(Coming down to earth)* Oh, God! Jessica...

He heads off in the other direction.

(calling) Jessica! Jessica! Jessica!

As he goes, the lights fade to a:

Blackout.

Scene Two

The same. A few days later.

Another morning. Another sunny day.

ALGY comes from the house. He stands in the fresh air for a moment, taking deep breaths prior to resuming work in the summerhouse.

As he does so, JESSICA enters from the far end of the garden. She has been picking flowers. She stops as she sees ALGY.

JESSICA Oh, hello, there... Can I help you at all?

ALGY Ah, good morning.

JESSICA Were you wanting someone?

ALGY What?

JESSICA Were you looking for anyone in particular?

ALGY No, Jess, it's me.

JESSICA Sorry?

ALGY It's me. Algy.

   JESSICA looks blank.

   Your husband. It's Algy.

JESSICA My – *(realising, bewildered)* Oh, heavens! Algy! Sorry, from this distance – without my... I mistook you for someone else.

ALGY *(gently humouring her)* Easy mistake to make.

JESSICA You're up bright and early.

ALGY Thought I'd make an early start. On the new one. Only just this minute come down.

JESSICA How are you getting on?

ALGY *(grimly)* Still stuck in the middle of chapter seventeen...

JESSICA Oh, dear. How awful. I'm so sorry.

ALGY Bloody frustrating, I can tell you...

JESSICA It must be.

ALGY Got this far with it... Stuck solid. Same point. Four days in a row. Can't get past it. I need a run at it. Can't get a run at it. How can I work up any head of steam, when people are continually distracting me...?

JESSICA Well, they should all know better by now, surely?

ALGY That journalist, a few days ago, didn't help. Then I had John Potting here all day Wednesday, clipping and pruning and – whatever he does out here – mulching...

JESSICA We can't begrudge him that, this garden's his pride and joy. We can hardly deny John his clipping and pruning, can we? The place would go completely wild. Besides, you know what he's like if you try to stop him, he'd get terribly moody...

ALGY I don't begrudge him his clipping and pruning, but I just wish to God he wouldn't stop every five minutes to tell me about it...

JESSICA Remember the time he was off sick for a fortnight, in the middle of July? You could barely find your way round out here, could you? Two weeks, that's all it took. It was like a rainforest. I was practically on the point of sending out search parties for you...

ALGY And then most of yesterday was taken up by that chap looking at the drain down the end there...

JESSICA Oh, that was a must. An absolute must. We couldn't have left it another day. Talk about you having blockages. This was really serious, I can tell you...

ALGY Yes, I heard all about that as well, thank you. From him. At great length and in lurid detail. The trouble is, these days, if

I get distracted, get talking about something irrelevant, like problems with the drains, I find it creeps into the writing. At her morning briefing, I found the Chief Super suddenly launching into a lengthy discourse on Grimthorpe's sewage system. Keeps happening lately. Don't know why. Age, I suppose.

JESSICA Yes. We all get a little confused occasionally. About what's real and what isn't, don't we? I know I do. And I'm not even writing a book.

ALGY How are you feeling today?

JESSICA Oh, much better, thank you. Very much better.

ALGY You gave us quite a scare the other day, you know, wandering off like that...

JESSICA *(a little embarrassed)* Yes, I did explain. There was a certain confusion.

ALGY I don't know what the people down the lane there must have thought. Finding you calmly sitting there in the middle of their back garden...

JESSICA Yes, I did explain, we do both have very similar back gates. It was an easy mistake to make, wasn't it?

ALGY *(unconvinced)* Oh, yes.

JESSICA Anyway, it would never have happened if they hadn't decided to move all the shops. Why on earth they wanted to move them, I have no idea. What was wrong with where they used to be? It was never a problem before, was it?

ALGY *(uneasily)* I'm sure they had good reason.

JESSICA Council planners! A law unto themselves, aren't they? I've a jolly good mind to write to the local paper, you know.

ALGY No, that's defunct, dear.

JESSICA What?

ALGY It's no longer printed. It's gone out of circulation.

JESSICA Since when? When did they decide to do that?

ALGY Oh, couple of years ago now.

JESSICA You can't keep up with things, can you? Everything's changing so fast, isn't it? Makes one almost breathless, in a way, don't you think?

ALGY Yes. Life's speeding up, we're slowing down. We're no longer enjoying the ride, just clinging on for dear life, wishing to God somebody'd take their bloody foot off the accelerator.

A pause.

(indicating her flowers) Those are pretty.

JESSICA *(aware she is holding them)* Oh. Yes. They're for the table. I thought we needed fresh ones. The ones last night were looking terribly droopy, I thought. I keep telling Mrs. Henshaw she must replace them on a regular basis but she never listens to a word I say. Whenever I make a suggestion, she just smiles and says, "Yes, dear." But then never does a thing about it.

ALGY *(barely listening)* Yes, dear...

JESSICA *(moving off)* Well. I must get on.

ALGY Yes, Thelma's due in a minute...

JESSICA Yes, I'll tell her not to disturb you, shall I?

ALGY You could try.

JESSICA How's her mother, by the way? I've been meaning to ask her.

ALGY *(shrugging)* Much the same, I understand. A gradual deterioration.

JESSICA *(smiling sadly)* Ah, well. It'll come to us all in the end, won't it?

ALGY *(somewhat depressed)* Yes.

JESSICA *(cheerily)* See you later, then. Happy writing!

She goes off to the house.

ALGY Thanks very much. *(taking his usual deep breath)* Here goes then! If at first you don't succeed... Take ten. Where were we?

He goes through his ritual of winding himself up as he prepares to start writing.

The lights return to the previous state with the accompanying background sounds.

TOMMY *wanders back, still deep in thought, to resume his previous position. The lights gradually dim to their nighttime state.*

(wearily re-reading as if for the umpteenth time) ...As Tommy stared morosely at the swings, miniature roundabouts and rusting slides, he was sharply reminded of another playground, not a dozen miles from there, where he and DCI Gilpin had made that fateful, grisly discovery...

GEMMA *re-enters with fresh drinks, a pint for him and another pink tonic for her.*

The pub sounds resume as before.

GEMMA *(as she enters, calling)* ...Here you are. One pint of horrible brew...

TOMMY *(re-entering, still deep in his thoughts)* Ta.

GEMMA He's cheeky that barman, isn't he?

TOMMY What? Giving you lip, was he?

GEMMA God's gift to women, he reckons.

TOMMY He's harmless enough is Harry.

GEMMA He better be. Lucky for him I had my hands full.

TOMMY He's all talk, Harry. We go back a long way, me and him. Cheers!

GEMMA Cheers! *(sitting back on the bench)* Now, then. Are you going to tell me about it? What you got against this bloke that's so personal?

TOMMY Oh, aye. Him.

A slight pause.

Sure you want to hear?

GEMMA Bursting.

TOMMY It's not pleasant –

GEMMA I'm comfortable with unpleasant.

TOMMY Well, ten years ago, one night in April, early evening, we got this shout from uniform. Something unusual in this garden, out at West Shale.

GEMMA What, the same one we were in –?

TOMMY Aye, the same one we've just been in. This were still a posh area even back in those days. Smart. Stockbrokers and that. Saucers with their cups. Any road, this householder next door she'd spotted something peculiar, in the adjoining garden. Something not quite right. Called it in. By the time we both got there, Reg and I, we found this...this... She was... this lass... *(shakes his head at the memory)* ...sixteen years old...strangled...lying there...her dress up round her...like so much discarded... You know what gets to you, finding something like that? Apart from the violence, the brutality... It's the – the disregard. The sheer disregard someone has for a fellow human being. Like they weren't even the same species.

GEMMA Well, they're not, are they? That sort. Not really.

TOMMY No, they're a subspecies. Lot of talk in the old days about Darwin and that. How he reckoned we separated from the apes. Major moment in the history of mankind. In my opinion, that weren't the only time we divided. It seems to me we been dividing and subdividing ever since it started. Doesn't ever get any better, either. Just keeps narrowing itself down. Till half the world's mindless lunatics, the other half's Stephen Hawking and Mother Teresa...

GEMMA Don't know where that puts us.

TOMMY *(with a gesture)* Somewhere just about between, love. In between.

GEMMA But you caught this bastard? This Leonard Arthur Hemp?

TOMMY Aye. We caught him. No problem there. He more or less owned up to it straightaway. Perfectly content to do that. Very happy to do so. Smiling, like it was some great game. Taking a girl like that out of the world. Destroying everyone around her, her parents, her friends, her family. A whole sodding community, broken in pieces. He even confessed. Sat there, delighted with himself. Have you ever met an evil man? That's what he is. Real evil. In the old-fashioned sense. You know, like in the Bible. Only way to describe him. He has this laugh, you know. Nothing to do with laughter, not as we know it. If you hear it, it freezes your blood, like. I sometimes imagine it's what his victims must hear, just before he kills them. Evil. All the time we were questioning him, I could feel Reg's fingers itching, you know, to get 'em round his throat. Give him a taste of what he'd done to that lass. I know that's how I felt. Still makes me come out in a sweat, thinking about it.

GEMMA So, what happened to change things? Open and shut case, I'd have thought? If he was that guilty?

TOMMY You'd have thought. As I said, money, love. Speaks louder than words, often. It's not silence that does that. It's money. Rich parents. Bloody hedge fund managers. He lawyered up. Brought in a top QC from down south, withdrew his confession. Claimed it'd been obtained under duress, physical coercion. We never so much as laid a finger on the bugger. Not that we didn't come close, mind. But, as I say, Reg Gilpin, he was always by the book. Wasn't in his nature. So, by the time Hemp found two or three convenient last-minute witnesses, all of them incidentally sporting nice shiny new cars, to provide him with a cast-iron alibi, plus the sudden mysterious unexplained absence of vital pieces of circumstantial evidence, Reg and I, from being cock-a-hoop at having caught the bugger, suddenly found the whole case collapsed round our ears. As a result, Leonard Arthur Hemp walked out of court a free man, still smiling broader than ever. Bastard!

GEMMA We'll nail him this time, guv. Providing he's back here.

TOMMY He's back. He's been down south for a while, apparently, hiding out in a boarding house in Eastbourne. But now he's back. He's that cocky, that pleased with himself. Thinks he got away with it. Mark my word, he'll be keen to prove himself, have another go. Another chance to make fools of us again. Only this time, ten years on, we'll be ready for him. He won't be laughing this time, that's for sure.

A slight pause.

(rising and moving off) Same again, is it?

GEMMA *(following him, alarmed)* No, guv, honestly. It's nearly closing. They'll be shutting up in a minute...

TOMMY I'll have a word with him, he'll stay open for me, will Harry...

GEMMA *(as they go off)* No, I must be getting home, really, guv...

TOMMY *(going off)* Harry owes me, love, he owes me one...

GEMMA ...This is my fifth late night in a row...

They both go off, still arguing.

ALGY Gemma conjectured that if Tommy Middlebrass employed a similar technique to interviewing suspects as he did to press-ganging publicans into illegally staying open after hours, then accusations of coercion levelled against him could not lightly be dismissed. As a result, two and a half hours and three unwanted glasses of pink tonic later, sober, if bloated and full-bladdered, DS Gemma Price finally made her way gratefully homewards to her bed.

He punches the air triumphantly.

The lights return to normal.

The pub sounds, which have peaked slightly over the last, now fade out.

End dictation. Yes! Gotcha! End of chapter seventeen! Ha!

He sits there feeling pleased with himself for a second.

THELMA *enters from the house with a copy of the newspaper. She has a slight air of tension and trepidation.*

THELMA *(nervously)* Algy! Algy!

ALGY Hello?

THELMA Is this a good moment? I hope I've chosen a good moment to interrupt?

ALGY Thelma, my dear, for once you have chosen an excellent moment. Chapter seventeen is finally completed.

THELMA Oh, good. I am pleased. It's been such a problem, hasn't it?

ALGY What can I do for you?

THELMA I thought you should see this straightaway.

She gingerly slides the copy of the newspaper onto his desk beside him.

I think you need to see it.

ALGY Ah! Is this the interview? It's in at last, then? The idiot finally managed to get it published, did he? *(taking the newspaper)* Let's have a look.

THELMA It's – towards the back.

ALGY Well, I hardly imagined it'd be on the front page.

He turns a few pages.

(casually passing a photo) Good God, what on earth's that woman wearing, I ask you? Or rather, not wearing?

He turns more pages. He pauses.

THELMA A bit further towards the back...

ALGY *turns yet more pages.*

No, still further. Keep going...

ALGY *(still turning pages)* Where the hell have they put it, then? I'll be in the bloody sports section at this rate. Don't tell me he's put me in the sports – Ah, here it is!

He stops as he reaches the page with his picture.

THELMA There!

ALGY Well, at least they've managed to print a decent-sized picture.

THELMA Yes.

ALGY Quite an old one though, isn't it? When on earth was that taken? At least thirty years ago...

THELMA At least.

ALGY *(starting to read the article)* Still, not a bad size, is it? Can't complain about column inches, I suppose... So, what's he say about me...

He starts to read silently, his lips barely moving.

THELMA *waits for the penny to drop.*

A silence.

Eventually, ALGY *stops reading.*

ALGY *(at last, slowly)* This is an obituary, isn't it? I'm reading my own obituary, aren't I? That fucking idiot's put me in the obituary column. *(getting more agitated)* What the hell am I doing reading my obituary, for Christ's sake? What am I doing in here? I'm not even dead! *(shouting)* I'm not even bloody dead, am I?

THELMA *(nervously)* No, no. You're very much alive, Algy.

ALGY To cap it all, it's not even accurate. He hasn't even got his facts right, has he? Going on and on about those stupid kids' books. Listen to this. *(reading)* "Popular author of the legendary *Silly Milly* series, beloved heroine for generations of children..." What is all this garbage?

THELMA I know, he's got it all terribly wrong, hasn't he? There's been the most awful confusion.

ALGY You're telling me there has –

THELMA Wires have got dreadfully crossed somewhere, that's all I can think.

ALGY It just goes on, column after column, about Silly Milly and Fucking Horace, doesn't it? Not a single mention of Middlebrass –

THELMA Well, he does mention the television series. Just briefly. At the end –

ALGY What about the books? Where does it mention the books? There are thirty-two of them. Thirty-three if you count this one. Not to mention about twenty-five other titles! It's unbelievable! It's bad enough reading your own obituary but when the stupid bastard hasn't even got it right...! I'm speechless. Ring the editor! Get him on the line, right away!

THELMA *(backing away)* Yes, of course. I'll see if I can get hold of him.

ALGY I want to speak to him in person, do you hear? To prove I'm still alive –

THELMA Yes. You don't think you'd be better talking to the person in charge of obituaries, do you? Rather than the editor himself. I mean, he might be rather busy...

ALGY What's more important than this?

THELMA I mean, there's rather a lot going on in the rest of the world at the moment, Algy, and he might have a lot on his plate, at present –

ALGY I don't care if World War Three's broken out, get him on the line, you hear? Personally! The editor-in-chief. In person. Understood?

THELMA Yes.

She makes to leave.

ALGY *(a sudden thought)* Oh, my God! My publishers! What are they going to think? Get hold of my publishers, as well. If they read this, they'll probably panic. They'll think they've lost their star author. Get hold of Jason Ratcliffe! Tell him not to panic!

THELMA Will do! *(just before she leaves)* It's a lovely final paragraph. You really ought to read it. It's terribly nice about you. Sweet.

She leaves him alone.

ALGY *sits and digests his altered circumstances.*

ALGY That's all I needed, all I needed. I'm still alive, aren't I? *(patting himself and feeling his pulse)*

He calms down slightly. In a moment, he picks up the newspaper and scans the offending article rapidly, shaking his head, irritated by what he's reading.

(reaching the final paragraph, reading) "...He was blessed with that rare mixture of a lively mind, a razor-sharp wit, combined with a mischievous spirit of adventure. At his public school, he rapidly gained the reputation as a legendary

wicket-keeper. Algy remained, to the end, a gentle, good-humoured, naturally modest, somewhat shy, family man. He was greatly loved by the select few fortunate to know him personally and, more widely, through his writings, will be remembered fondly by everyone for years to come."

He is practically moved to tears by this and blinks somewhat to try and contain them.

(smiling) "...He will be remembered fondly by everyone for years to come." That's nice.

JESSICA *enters, as before, with more flowers.*

JESSICA *(seeing* **ALGY***)* Oh, hello there! You've managed to fix it, I see?

ALGY *(puzzled)* Sorry?

JESSICA Our wretched drain, I see you've managed to fix it. Well done! My husband will be absolutely delighted! Well done!

She goes out.

ALGY *(glaring after her, bitterly)* That's a bloody good start, I must say.

As he sits gloomily, the lights fade to a:

Blackout.

ACT II

Scene One

The same. Two days later.

As at the start of Act I, the garden is in darkness with ALGY *in his summerhouse.*

TOMMY, *followed by* GEMMA, *creeps on.*

GEMMA *(sotto, anxiously as they enter)* ...I still think we should be calling for backup, guv, I really do.

TOMMY *(sotto, grimly)* I've told you, lass, this is between me and him. Me and Leonard Arthur Hemp. Face-to-face and personal –

GEMMA No point in putting your life in danger, is there, just to settle a –?

TOMMY Listen, I said, you don't have to come with me. No obligation. You're free to go any time, just leave me to it –

GEMMA How could I possibly leave now? Be sensible, guv...

TOMMY Suit yourself, then.

GEMMA What if that witness was right and he has got hold of a firearm from somewhere? What then?

TOMMY He's not going to use it. He's not going to use a gun. That's not his way, not Leonard Arthur Hemp. Not how he works. He'll weasel his way out. I know how his devious, twisted little mind works. Shooting me, that's never going to happen. Not his way.

GEMMA How can you be certain?

TOMMY Look, if he shoots me, as far as he's concerned, that's game over, isn't it? Finish? Kaput? In his mind, he's lost, I've won.

GEMMA You've won?

TOMMY That's the way he'll see it.

GEMMA By being dead? You'll have won, even though you're dead?

TOMMY Right.

GEMMA And he'll have lost?

TOMMY Technically. In his mind, he will have done. That's the way I reckon it.

GEMMA Don't tell me, it's in your water?

TOMMY No.

GEMMA In your nose, then? Your copper's nose?

TOMMY No. Not there either. *(tapping his head)* It's here. Sixth sense.

GEMMA I can't keep up with you. I tell you, they never taught us any of this at college.

TOMMY They won't have. It can't be taught. It's what's known as innate. Innate policing.

GEMMA *(muttering)* Insane policing, more like.

TOMMY You can mock, girl, you can mock. Tell me, have I ever steered you wrong?

GEMMA Always a first time.

TOMMY Come on then, he's not back yet, we'll wait in the car.

GEMMA Wait for what?

TOMMY *(starting to move back)* Until he's back. Catch him red-handed then. Finally nail him, this time...

GEMMA (*following him*) But what about the hostage? Remember, he's left a hostage in there, hasn't he?

TOMMY She's safe enough for now...

They go off again. The lights return to the daylight state during the next.

ALGY (*resuming his narration*) They returned to the car, parked in its usual spot, concealed behind the thick hawthorn hedge in the lane, just beyond the back gate. They sat in the darkness, waiting and watching, as the condensation gradually built up on the windows, amidst the lingering odour of last night's tandoori takeaway. Waiting, once again, for Hemp. For the return of Leonard Arthur Hemp. Despite Tommy's reassurances, Gemma's thoughts kept returning to Hemp's young victim, the luckless Peggy Jenkins, imprisoned somewhere in that vast looming house, alone and terrified in the darkness. What an ordeal it must have been for the girl, Gemma reflected. One minute, innocently going about her normal routine serving in the village store and the next, from all accounts, snatched violently at gunpoint. Gemma shuddered to think of the gamble she and Tommy were taking with the girl's life by choosing not to rush in to the rescue but instead wait for her captor to return. What if they missed the moment? Failed to catch Hemp red-handed at the last minute, as they planned? Missed their chance altogether, abandoning her to the cruel mercies of Hemp? What then? What then? Dot. Dot. Dot, question mark. End of chapter twenty-five. End dictation.

He pauses for breath.

(*pleased, to himself*) Good! Good! That's good. Cliff-hanger. It's all cooking nicely. Nearly there. (*doing a little fanfare*) Tara! Taraaaa!

THELMA *enters to catch the end of this.*

THELMA Ah! Is that a good noise, I hear?

ALGY Taraaaa! End of chapter twenty-five! Nailed the bugger at last!

THELMA Oh, good. Is there much more to go, do you think?

ALGY I reckon just one more. I should be able to wrap it up in one. Rescue the girl, shaken but unharmed, and finally kill off Leonard Arthur Hemp, whom I must say I've grown rather fond of over the four books he's featured in –

THELMA Oh, I don't care for Hemp at all, not at all. Very unpleasant, with that sinister laugh. Anyone who does that to a little dog like he did in the last book loses all my sympathy.

ALGY No matter he'd also killed a defenceless girl before he did so...?

THELMA Oh, well, what else do you expect from a serial killer? That's only to be expected. But I did find the dog particularly shocking for some reason. I know one or two people agreed with me, too, judging from the online comments...

ALGY I'm sure they did. Most people in this country put dogs before people.

THELMA Well dogs have no choice, do they?

ALGY People don't have that much either. If a complete stranger decides to murder you unexpectedly he's hardly going to turn up in advance with a bloody questionnaire, is he? You know, that's what I value most about you, Thelma. Your sheer averageness – invaluable. If I need to know how most people are going to react to something, no need for costly surveys or lengthy market research. I need look no further than you, my dear. You're what, in bygone days, used to be known by publishers as the Man on the Clapham Omnibus...

THELMA I'm not sure quite how to take that. That makes me sound rather common...

ALGY Nothing wrong in common.

THELMA No?

ALGY At least most people share your opinion.

THELMA No, I'm getting very confused by all this. How do you plan to kill Hemp off, then?

ALGY I don't know, I haven't decided yet. Possibly a fire? Maybe he accidentally sets fire to the house and burns to death?

THELMA In terrible agony?

ALGY Oh, yes! Excruciating. But then I've used fire rather a lot recently, haven't I?

THELMA That's how you killed the serial rapist?

ALGY Jonty Weller... Now he was nasty. Deeply nasty.

THELMA And the head of that paedophile ring, he went the same way, didn't he?

ALGY Oh, yes, of course. Craig Gibbons. Yes, I've set fire to quite a number of my villains, one way or another, haven't I?

THELMA They all thoroughly deserved it, too. I think of it as symbolically burning them in the fires of hell...

ALGY Purely intentional, of course. No, I think Leonard Arthur probably dies in a fall. Also symbolic...

THELMA Down the main staircase?

ALGY Or out of a window?

THELMA Impaled on some sharp railings?

ALGY (shaking his head) No, it'll come to me. I'll have a think. Did you want something?

THELMA Sorry?

ALGY When you came out just now? Did you want me for something?

THELMA Oh, yes, sorry. Your publisher phoned. He's en route apparently.

ALGY Jason? Coming up by train, is he? Or is he driving?

THELMA Neither. By helicopter, apparently.

ALGY Helicopter?

THELMA He was somewhere over Leicestershire when he rang. He is planning to land just outside the village. He'll be here – *(consulting her watch)* – oh, heavens – any minute!

ALGY Why the hell's he coming by helicopter? What's wrong with the train, like everyone else?

THELMA Maybe he felt it was urgent? Perhaps he was in a hurry to sort things out for you?

ALGY It's taken him two days even to agree to come here, he couldn't have felt it was that urgent. Old Joe Ratcliffe, his father, always used to travel here by coach. Took him two days to get here but at least he wasn't needlessly wasting his client's cash, unlike his boneheaded son.

THELMA He's always very pleasant on the phone with me. As I say, he sounded anxious to get this obituary business sorted out.

ALGY By the way, have you had any reaction from the website?

THELMA *(guardedly)* Not – a great amount, no.

ALGY You're positive you published the denial? Told the world I'm still alive?

THELMA Yes, it was difficult to put into simple words, though. *(laughing)* I did consider quoting Mark Twain: "Reports of my death have been greatly exaggerated," but I felt that could sound a little frivolous, under the circumstances.

ALGY Would have done the trick.

THELMA Well, quite honestly, these days, we get so little traffic, compared to what we used to. Less and less followers as the years go by. I think most of them are most probably – terrible thing to say – but I think most of them have probably passed on, frankly. They're all your age or even older. The young people we attract these days seem to be focusing on the *Silly Milly* section. That seems to be much our busiest area, currently –

ALGY That's still on there? *Silly Milly*? I told you to take that rubbish down.

THELMA It's not rubbish, Algy, it really isn't. You mustn't say that. Run your own work down. It's proving terribly popular with younger people, especially young parents. And the numbers are steadily growing, day by day. It's very exciting to think you're getting a new young readership, especially at your age –

ALGY In their eyes, I'm so old they'll probably assume I'm dead anyway.

THELMA Algy, you're so depressing! You really are!

ALGY Half the world believes I'm dead and the other half presumes I must be.

THELMA Well, that is depressing, when you put it like that.

A helicopter flying very loudly and low suddenly passes overhead, causing them both to duck instinctively.

THELMA That's probably him.

ALGY Flamboyant bastard. That's my money he's burning up there.

A silence.

Where's Jessica? She hasn't gone walkabout again, has she?

THELMA The last time I saw her she was by the French windows looking out here.

ALGY What was she looking at?

THELMA Well – you.

ALGY Me?

THELMA She was asking who you were. What you were doing out here in the summerhouse. I'm afraid she's forgotten who you are again, Algy. I keep reminding her, too. I mean, she seems to recognise me and Mrs. Henshaw most of the time and she even knows who Mr. Potting is occasionally. But I think she does have terrible difficulty remembering who you are, for some reason. I'm so sorry. It must be so hurtful for you. After all these years of being together. I know a little of how you must feel. My mother has absolutely no idea most of the time who I am these days, either.

ALGY *(depressed, thoughtfully)* Well. Jess was never that fond of me. Even in the early days, when we were both supposedly in love. I don't think she was terribly fond of me even then.

THELMA I'm sure that's not true.

ALGY She never showed it.

THELMA And did you? To her?

Before **ALGY** *can reply, the sound of a distant bell from the house.*

That's him. Are you ready?

ALGY As I'll ever be.

THELMA I'll fetch him, then. I presume you'll talk to him out here, won't you?

ALGY Sure, bring him out.

THELMA *goes off to the house.*

ALGY *goes through another version of his welcoming routine.*

(laughing delightedly) Jason! Jason, mate!

He forces his reluctant face into the same ghastly smile as before.

(pacing) Ha-ha! Ha-ha-ha! Well, well, well, well, well! Aha! Ha-ha! *(tiring)* Not a patch on his father. Half the man. Incompetent. Triple C smoothie. All cologne, cashmere and charisma.

THELMA *enters with* JASON.

ALGY'*s description of him is reasonably accurate.*

JASON, *by default, directs a lot of his charm towards* THELMA, *who, unaccustomed to this barrage of male attention, becomes a little flustered.*

THELMA Here we are, just out here.

ALGY *(ecstatically)* Jason, old mate!

JASON *(likewise)* Algy! Dear fellow!

ALGY My dear chap! How goes it?

JASON Just flew straight over you, did you see us? In the 'copter?

ALGY Oh, that was you up there, was it?

JASON *(laughing)* You could at least have waved.

ALGY Wasn't sure it was you. There's so many people flying by in helicopters these days, don't want to start waving to complete strangers, do we?

He laughs.

JASON *(laughing with him)* No, you'll have to excuse the mode of transport but don't blame me if you live so far off the beaten path, old boy. Where the hell are we anyway? I forget. The pilot did tell me.

THELMA North Yorkshire. The Esk Valley.

JASON Beautiful. *(looking around, to* THELMA*)* Well this is a bijou BKS, I must say.

THELMA BKS?

JASON Best Kept Secret, sweetie. Stunning from up there.

THELMA It's even lovelier from down here.

JASON So I can see, sweetie.

THELMA Thelma.

JASON You're here year-round, Algy, I take it?

ALGY Oh, yes, all year.

JASON I don't think I could quite manage that, you know. Come November, I sense I'd be overwhelmed by the urge to make a quick bolt for civilisation.

THELMA Oh, it's not been too bad, lately. We've had one or two harsh winters but generally the weather hasn't been too bad. Not like the old days –

JASON No, I was thinking more of a social life. I imagine during the winter months, this joint isn't exactly jumping socially, is it, sweetie?

THELMA *(laughing)* Thelma. Oh, no, hardly jumping, no...

ALGY We're happy enough to avoid civilisation, whenever possible. Or what passes for civilisation, these days.

JASON Yes, you always were a bit of a recluse, Algy, weren't you? *(winking to* THELMA*)* Still, these writers, sweetie. We must make allowances, mustn't we?

THELMA *(smiling)* Thelma.

JASON It takes all sorts, doesn't it? We have this one chap, permanently lives in a penthouse on the top floor of a hotel slap in the middle of WC1. Never leaves the place except for meals. Got his own little garden. High-level patio complete with barbecue. Even has his own swimming pool. All up there on the seventy-somethingth. High life or what, eh?

THELMA He must be very successful.

JASON In spades, sweetie, in spades. Most of his stuff – straight to movies. Movies or mini-series. Megabucks, believe me. *(winking)* Megabucks.

ALGY *(smiling)* Good for him.

JASON *(smiling)* Good for all of us, eh?

ALGY Especially you.

JASON *(smiling)* You betcha. He writes complete and utter garbage, of course, but who am I to complain, if it keeps me in clean knickers, eh? But I can tell you, it's great to get up here for a change, away from the burly hurly, hobnobbing with you serious chaps for a change.

A pause.

THELMA Can I offer you a – coffee, perhaps?

JASON Something long and cool and tempting would be perfect, sweetie.

THELMA A glass of water?

JASON *(smiling)* I was thinking of something a trifle more tempting than that. If you have a spot of wine, that'd go down a treat.

THELMA Wine. Right.

JASON White.

THELMA White.

JASON And, sweetie...

THELMA Thelma. Yes?

JASON If it could have just a touch of fizz to it, I'd be greatly appreciative...

THELMA *(momentarily confused)* Fizz? Oh, I see, *fizz.* Yes. *(to* ALGY, *slightly panicked)* Do we have any – fizz?

ALGY In the cellar.

THELMA Cellar. Yes.

ALGY At the back. There's some Prosecco.

THELMA Prosecco.

JASON Perfect. Thank you so much, sweetie, sorry to put you to so much trouble.

THELMA Thelma, yes. That's quite all right, it's no trouble.

She goes off.

JASON *(gazing after her)* She's a poppet, isn't she? Perfect little sweetie.

From his pocket, his mobile rings.

(making to answer it) Sorry, chum. Must take this. Promised to let them know the minute I'd arrived. If the little darlings lose sight of me for ten seconds, straight into headless chicken mode. *(answering)* Hi... Hi, sweetie...yep...yep... No problems, no... Very smooth... *(laughing uproariously)* No! ...No! ...Not at all, none of that, sweetie, not at that altitude, no... Yep! ...Yep! Talk to you later, sweetie... Yep! ...Will do... Roger and out! *(rings off)* Sorry. That's my little Carlotta. Absolute duckie.

ALGY She sounds it.

JASON Well, I'm relieved to see you're still up and about and breathing God's good air, old boy. It was quite alarming to read your obituary the other day, I must say.

ALGY Fairly alarming for me, too.

JASON *(roaring with laughter)* Must have been! Must have been! I can well imagine! Quite a good final write-up, though, didn't you think? As obituaries go?

ALGY It was appalling.

JASON Really? You thought so?

ALGY He got every single bloody fact wrong. Amazing he even got the name right. More than he could manage during the interview.

JASON Yes, well, I gather, as obituary writers go, he's a bit of a second-stringer. Reserves bench, you know. I understand most of them don't regularly choose to take his stuff if they can avoid it. A lot of it as you say is, by all accounts, wildly inaccurate. Tends to somewhat jumble his facts, according to reliable sources. Had a major dustup a few years back with George Clooney's people... But I gather, in your particular case, there was a genuine mix-up. The interview he did with you got filed in the wrong tray, apparently. Ended up in the obits instead. That being his usual line. So they knocked it into some sort of shape and just put it out verbatim, without checking.

ALGY They must have realised it was an interview, for God's sake?

JASON Clearly not. They rarely read these things through thoroughly, you know. They turned it round, shoved it all in the past-tense, changed all the "is's" to "was's," that sort of thing. Major cock-up, of course. Red faces and damp underwear all round. Still, no lasting damage, was there?

ALGY You think not?

JASON No publicity is the only bad publicity and all that. It might just have sold you another couple of copies, you never know your luck.

ALGY And did it?

JASON No, not really, I'm afraid. Not a single one. Sadly. Zilch.

A pause.

Which is why I really wanted to come and have a word with you, old boy. I don't have to tell you, of all people, you've been in this game as long as anyone, longer than most of us, I don't have to tell you, that the publishing lark these days is a constantly moving vehicle. Step away from it for a split-second and it's left you standing at the bus stop, it's already halfway down the next street and moving away fast. And so you constantly need to keep moving with it. You get my gist?

ALGY Whereas I haven't? I'm still at the bus stop. Is that what you're saying?

JASON Last week, I popped downstairs to accounts and had a quick shufty. Frankly, your sales figures are static, old boy. Pickled in aspic. Cast adrift in formaldehyde. Your last couple of efforts – well, they've barely covered the cost of the endpapers.

ALGY I see.

A pause.

JASON *(gently)* I assume you must have been aware of the state of things from your royalty statements – or rather lack of them?

ALGY *(rallying)* You don't – you don't feel that it would have helped the sales if my last two books had had any sort of promotion at all, do you?

JASON How do you mean?

ALGY *(getting angrier)* I mean, I see all your other clients, living fifty floors up, having their bloody books plugged here there and everywhere. Dozens of reviews, endless puffs on radio chat shows, breakfast time TV, back pages of the supplements. They get mentioned everywhere, don't they? But I haven't seen a single mention of my last two – *Death Down the Line* or *Murder Mistook* – where the hell were they? No mention of them anywhere. Not a dicky bird. Even the mobile library here had never heard of them. Did you ever make the slightest attempt to sell either of them?

JASON *(taken aback by this onslaught)* Ah, now, Algy, to be fair –

ALGY Or even before that? What about *Death Comes Quickly* or *The Weeping Corpse*? Or *The Case of the Cautious Samaritan*? When was there a single mention of any of those?

JASON Now, Algy, old boy, steady –

ALGY Or earlier? What about *Strangle Me With Kindness*? *Murder or Your Money Back* –? You want me to go through the whole bloody list, do you? All thirty-three of the fucking things?

JASON Algy, Algy, old chap! Please! Steady! Whoa, old boy! Easy!

ALGY *(pausing for breath)* Well, then.

JASON Dear chap, simmer down. *(in an attempt to calm him)* Thirty-three. Have you really written thirty-three of them?

What a terrific achievement! I had no idea there were so many...

ALGY You've published them all, you should know. Actually, there are thirty-two. I'm currently working on thirty-three...

JASON Oh, really? Oh, there's a new one, is there? What's this one called, then? Has it got a title, yet?

ALGY It's called *Second Time Lucky*.

JASON Ah, yes. This'll be another in the saga, I take it? Your detective series? Inspector Fortinbras?

ALGY Middlebrass.

JASON Middlebrass. That's the chap! He's been going for ages, hasn't he? Must be about a hundred and twelve by now. Older than Hercule Poirot. About due for his police pension by now, isn't he? I used to adore the television series when I was a kid. Glued to the box, week after week. Wonderful stuff. Still remember them. Remember your detective, Middlebrow, slamming the door, facing up to the villain. *(in a faintly dodgy Welsh accent)* "Now, then, boyo, it's high time you and me had a little chat, innit?" *(laughs)* Yes.

ALGY *is ominously silent.*

You know, oddly enough, I never got round to reading the actual books themselves, for some reason. Bit like the James Bond ones. Never read those either. Like most people, I suppose, I went straight to movies.

Another slight pause.

Thirty-three! My God! That must be some sort of record, Algy, surely? You must be challenging Edgar Wallace, you must be?

ALGY *(grimly)* No, Edgar Wallace wrote over a hundred and seventy.

JASON Gracious! Well, you learn something new every day, don't you?

ALGY I don't imagine he had any particular problem selling
his books.

JASON No, I don't imagine he did. I know it must be
disappointing for you. After your long association with –
Fortin– Middlebrass, but as I say I think, sadly in this case
the vehicle's moved on, old boy. It's not even in the next
street. It's probably in the next town by now. *(taking a
breath)* What this is all leading up to, Algy, and I'm trying
to think of the nicest way to put this – because I sense this
is going to be painful for both of us – but I had a word with
our board last week, long before all this obituary nonsense
came up, you understand, and we came to the more or less
unanimous conclusion, that we ought to part company, you
and us. That we could no longer afford to publish you. That
we take you off our list.

A silence.

It's purely sordid finance, Algy, that's what it all boils down
to, these days. The tainted shilling. The filthy lucre. Quality?
Literary style? Technical ability? Forget all that. As for Art,
don't even mention the word. It's all money, money, money.
Sickening, sometimes. There are days, I can tell you, I sit in
my office I'm overcome with waves of nausea. No literally,
Algy, I kid you not. Deep down in my gut here. Thinking of
what's happened to us. Of what's left of Ratcliffe's. What used
to be Ratcliffe's, anyway. Of what Joe my father, Jeremiah,
my grandfather, had built up, through a genuine love and
passion for the business. Now look at us. Battered by a
succession of takeovers from a series of foreign philistines
with not an iota of appreciation for literature. I mean they
simply have no comprehension for quality writers like
yourself. They simply haven't. I was looking back on some
of your early reviews, Algy. *The Times* Lit Sup comparing
you to Dickens and Tolstoy. Which I suppose might have
been a trifle OTT even for *The Times* Lit. But, God, you're
part of the great English tradition, old boy. Austen. Harry
Fielding, Charlie Dickens, Tony Trollope... And now...Algy
Waterbridge.

Another silence.

ALGY *is making him sweat for it.*

(getting angrier, in his own way) No, be honest, Algy, it hasn't all been one-sided, now has it? Be fair. You did lead my poor late daddy, God rest his soul, one hell of a dance back then, didn't you? Be honest. All that trouble with the BBC in the sixties. Astronomic viewing figures, for the time, huge future prospects, everything going for you. Then in the middle of a third record-breaking series, you turn round and tell them all to get stuffed. I mean, how does that stack up with anything? You not only jumped ship, Algy, you then turned round and torpedoed the thing. All for some half-arsed detective series. Which, naturally, the BBC promptly abandoned and launched straight into *Z Cars*. Which, of course, went on to run forever. And then you had all those years of litigation, accusing every successful author in the book from John le Carré to Lee Child to J.K. Rowling of stealing your original ideas. Ending up in interminable, fruitless, prohibitive lawsuits. All of which you lost, I may add. And, throughout all that, to be fair, he stood by you, my father. Joe stood firmly in your corner holding the towel and clutching your gumshield, Algy, didn't he? Though, by the end, I do know he felt increasingly like the barman on the Titanic calling for last orders. Nonetheless he stood by you. Not just morally, either. Very often with his own money. Rashly, in my view. To use a currently fashionable phrase, Algy, your literary career has been one long suicide note from start to finish, hasn't it? So, I imagine reading your own obituary can't have come as that much of a surprise to you, can it?

Another silence.

No, I didn't mean to say that last bit... Sorry. Look, I'm sorry to bring such...that I had to... In this way... I'd hoped we could have...somehow... I'm really sorry, old mate, I really am. Yep.

A pause.

ALGY *(in full Middlebrass, gradually building in volume)* You should know, first, I've never been a mate of yours. I've never liked you, ever since you were a fat snotty little brat, stealing off your mother and breaking your father's heart. Been any justice, he hadn't died so sudden-like, you'd never have taken over from him. Been any justice, it should have been your sister took over, she's twice the man you are. You're crap at you job, what you know about publishing wouldn't cover a piece of paper I could wipe me arse on. You're a shallow, conceited, self-interested, pretentious, ignorant, chauvinist prick and if I'd been your dad I'd have taken my bloody belt off and thrashed you so hard you couldn't sit down for a month, lad. Now why don't you bugger off back to your fucking whirlybird before I tell you what I really think of you, eh?

JASON *is, for once, lost for words.*

JASON *(at length, recovering)* My father warned me about this. When he first brought me into the firm, he said to me, publishing's a wonderful business to be in, son, it's so rewarding. Its only drawback is having to deal with fucking authors.

A silence.

(finally) Goodbye, then.

He moves briskly to the door. As he does so, he nearly collides with **THELMA**, *who is carrying, with difficulty, a tray with two half-poured glasses of Prosecco, together with the bottle in a freezer sleeve.*

THELMA *(as she enters)* Whoops! Sorry.

JASON *(in a hurry, passing her)* Sorry!

THELMA *(startled)* Where are you going?

JASON *(hurrying away)* Sorry, sweetie, I have to dash – sorry.

He has left.

THELMA *(vainly, after him)* But I've only just this minute opened – oh. He hasn't really gone, has he? Have you both had words? Algy? What have you been saying? Oh, I see. We've had another visit from DCI Middlebrass, have we? I see.

A silence. ALGY *is clearly still recovering.*

Well, I don't know what I'm supposed to do with all this. This – fizz.

During the next, she places the tray and its contents on the table.

It took me ages to find it, it was right at the back behind the Bollinger. And then, once I'd found it, I had the most terrible trouble trying to open it. And when I finally did manage to, most of it sprayed all over the kitchen floor. So I had to mop that up, of course. It was like an ice rink. I was terrified someone might slip.

ALGY *does not respond.*

He's really upset you, Algy, hasn't he? What's he said to you? Is it something I should know about?

ALGY *(in a low voice)* They want shot of me.

THELMA Shot of you?

ALGY They no longer wants to publish me.

THELMA *(shocked)* Oh, Algy! How terrible!

ALGY Thank you and goodnight.

THELMA They can't, they simply can't. After all these years. They can't, surely?

ALGY They're perfectly within their rights.

THELMA After all your loyalty to them? Just like that? Well, you should sue them. Take them to court and sue them for compensation. For loss of earnings.

ALGY Apparently, I no longer have any earnings...

THELMA *(distressed for him)* Oh, Algy! We can't just leave it like that. There must be something we can do. Something.

ALGY We could start by drinking this, I suppose. That'd be a good start. That's what Tommy would do. Supposing he could even stomach this stuff. *(picking up a glass)* Here's looking at you, sunshine.

THELMA No, I can't possibly drink that, not at this time of day...

ALGY Oh, come on...

THELMA ...Not at any time of day, come to that...

ALGY ...Help me out with it. Help me out with the bottle, as Joe Ratcliffe used to say. In the old days, whenever we finished a meeting, he used to magically produce this bottle of single malt. Algy, old boy, help me out with this, will you? I can't count the bottles I helped Joe out with, over the years. Probably what killed him, most likely. Your good health, Thelma, my dear. To better times.

THELMA *(raising her glass)* To better times. *(suddenly overcome, tearfully)* Oh dear, I feel so terribly sad. I think I'm going to cry in a minute...

ALGY Oh, God's sake, don't cry, woman...

THELMA *(fighting back her tears)* Sorry...

ALGY – You start me off, as well... Look, drink that, you'll feel better...

THELMA ...So sorry... *(pulling herself together, then sipping her glass tentatively)* Oh, yes, it's really quite nice, isn't it?

ALGY Of course it's quite nice. It's very nice indeed.

THELMA *(savouring it)* I think I could develop a taste for this, in time.

ALGY Better lock the wine cellar, then.

The helicopter passes overhead in the other direction.

They both look up.

THELMA *(shouting at it, with uncharacteristic savagery)* Good riddance and sod off, sweetie!

ALGY *(mildly amused)* Now, now, language!

THELMA Odious man. Fancy working for him. *(suddenly remembering)* Oh, yes, I checked the computer just now whilst I was fighting with that bottle. I thought there may be something online that might help me with the cork. But then I saw our website had gone completely mad –

ALGY How do you mean?

THELMA With hits. Hit after hit! Constantly! Hundreds! Probably thousands, for all I know, I haven't had time to check the total.

ALGY Probably celebrating the obituary. Thank God the bugger's dead.

THELMA Oh, Algy, why can't you ever look on the bright side?

ALGY Because there isn't one. I spent my entire life looking for a bright side, Thelma, I've looked everywhere. And take it from me there isn't one. Despite all that the Pollyannas, Holy Joes and do-gooders might say to the contrary, if you think it's dark now, folks, wait till you see what's ahead of you.

THELMA *(putting down her glass)* Oh, dear, you're going into one of your moods again, aren't you? I can't bear to stand here listening to you sinking into one of your moods, Algy, not at the moment, I'm sorry. Not while I'm drinking this. It'll just get me more depressed and then I'll start worrying about Mother, I know I will. *(moving away)* I'm going to check the website, see how we're doing.

ALGY *(pouring himself another glass)* Right.

THELMA You – won't drink too much more of that, will you, Algy?

ALGY *(mildly irritated)* No...

THELMA Promise me. Promise?

ALGY *(sharply)* Yes!

THELMA And don't drink mine, either. I may come back for it.

She goes out.

ALGY *sips his glass, drains it and then defiantly pours himself another.*

He stares at his laptop, sighs and then sits at the keyboard once again.

ALGY Right. Here we go. Final lap. Chapter twenty-six.

He goes through his preparation ritual once again, winding himself up to start writing.

The lights fade down once again to their nighttime state during the next.

It was more than two hours later before their vigil was finally over when at long last they saw the figure of Leonard Arthur Hemp backlit by the village street lights, tottering drunkenly towards them along the lane, clutching what appeared to be, from what they could see through the car's misted-up windscreen, a supermarket bag of provisions. At least, thought Gemma, he was bringing home food, some of it hopefully intended to feed his victim. Hemp had clearly not yet finished with Peggy Jenkins but intended keeping her alive a little longer. She had a few more dark, miserable hours left to live. Tommy signalled they should wait a few more moments to allow Hemp to enter his front door before they made a move. And so the endless wait continued, until Middlebrass finally deemed it safe. Cautiously, they crept back across the lane, through the back gate into the pitch-dark garden.

TOMMY, *followed by* **GEMMA**, *creeps on as before.*

GEMMA *(as they enter, sotto)* What now? What's next in your master plan?

TOMMY *(sotto)* The master plan now, Detective Sergeant Price, as you sarcastically put it, is you wait here whilst I go a bit closer and call him out.

GEMMA Call him out?

TOMMY Get the bugger to show himself.

GEMMA Think that'll work?

TOMMY We'll see, won't we? I have a feeling he's that full of himself, he'll welcome the opportunity. Finally prove who's boss, him or me.

GEMMA What are the odds? Who do you reckon, then?

TOMMY Me, love. Money's on me, every time.

GEMMA Thought it might be.

TOMMY Wait on. Don't move.

He moves towards the house.

He stops some way short of it.

(shouting) Leonard! Lenny! Leonard Arthur Hemp! I know you're in there. Let the lass go and come out here, Lenny, if you've got the bottle. Act like a real man, for a change. Stop bullying defenceless lasses and come and face a proper man, if you dare. Come on, you bastard, I'm an old git, too, a bloody pensioner, aren't I? Or do you not fancy your chances against old folk either, is that it? Just young kids is it? Is that all you're good for, Lenny? Just a bloody coward Hemp, a snivelling coward at heart, aren't you?

ALGY Suddenly, high above them, they caught sight of movement.

GEMMA *(pointing)* Tommy! Look, up there on the roof! Look!

ALGY Silhouetted against the skyline, they could discern the outlines of two figures, the diminutive form of Peggy Jenkins together with Hemp himself, gripping the luckless girl by the back of her thin neck. Gemma held her breath as the two balanced precariously on the narrow ledge, high above them.

TOMMY *(looking up)* Oh, there you are. Come out at last have you, Lenny? That's where you're hiding. Still frightened to come face-to-face, are you? Still need to shelter behind a girl, do you? Come on, let her go, Lenny. Let go of the lass, why don't you? Frightened she'll smack you, is that it? Frightened she'll smack your bum, are you? Like your mum should have done, years ago? Should have brought you up proper, Lenny, shouldn't she? Come on, let her go!

ALGY In response, Hemp, emitting a mirthless, chilling laugh, abruptly released the girl, causing her to totter perilously close to the edge.

The sound of Hemp's laughter from above.

TOMMY Oh, yes, that's funny that is, that's really funny, Lenny, nearly fell then, didn't she? Peggy! Peggy, love, can you hear me? Now, Peggy, listen carefully, love. I see he's tied your hands but I want you to be very brave, darling. Can you be brave for me, Peggy? I want you very slowly to work your way back to that little door behind you, the one you just came through, all right? Can you do that for me, Peggy? Good girl. If you can manage to open it, as soon as you're through, I want you to make your way downstairs as quick as you can, out the front door and wait in the lane. Can you do that for me, love? You wait there for my colleague here, DS Price, Gemma. She'll take care of you from there. You're safe now, Peggy, no one's gonna hurt you, love. Off you go, carefully now, carefully. Ignore him, ignore that bugger. He can't hurt you, not anymore.

ALGY Gemma watched as Peggy gradually inched her way, her hands bound tightly behind her, past Hemp, step by tentative step. A thin figure, in her inadequate, flimsy summer dress, making agonisingly slow progress.

TOMMY *(watching her)* Well done love, that's it. That's it! You made it, well done! Off you go, now. Quick as you can. Now, Lenny, just you and me, eh?

GEMMA, *meanwhile, moving back, mirroring the offstage Peggy's progress, finally makes her way off the way she came and exits.*

TOMMY *remains motionless, still staring up at the unseen Hemp.*

(calling) Come on, then. What you waiting for, Lenny? You coming down to me, then, lad? Or do you want me to come up there to you? Is that what you want? Right, then, I'm game.

He moves slowly and remorselessly forward towards Hemp. Presumably, Hemp is doing the same, only more cautiously.

(as he moves) Here I come, then. Come on then, big fella! Fancy jumping then? I don't rate your chances from that height, lad, I don't at all. Here's where I come for you. It's payback time, Lenny, payback! For what you did to those lasses. The pain and misery you put them through, you little bastard.

Hemp's laughter is heard again.

What's that? Another joke, is it? Oh, we are having fun, aren't we? What's that you've got there, then? *(laughing)* Oh, if you're thinking of using that, Lenny, you'd better think again, lad. I tell you, you'll never hit me from up there, not from that angle. The odds on your hitting me from up there, shooting down, in the pitch dark, would take a better marksman than you'll ever be in –

From the roof, a pistol shot.

TOMMY's *body twitches as he is hit.*

He stands motionless for a moment.

Then he staggers back slightly.

TOMMY *(stunned with shock)* You bugger, you fluky little bugger. You shot me! You've been and bloody shot me, haven't you? *(beginning to feel the pain)* Oh, you bugger, you little bugger...

He staggers slightly as if dizzy and ends sitting heavily on the bench, as his life starts to slip away.

GEMMA *comes rushing back.*

GEMMA Tommy? *(seeing him)* Tommy! Tommy! You all right? What happened, guv? What's happened?

She hastily sits beside him on the bench.

TOMMY *(dazed)* He shot me. The little bugger shot me!

ALGY Tommy Middlebrass felt his life gradually start to slip away from him. After witnessing so many needless violent deaths over his long career, was this how death felt, thought Tommy?

GEMMA *(incredulous)* What do you mean, he shot you? *(shouting up at Hemp)* You can't shoot him! This is Tommy Middlebrass, you can't shoot him. Go on then! Go on, I dare you! Jump! Jump, you bugger, go on, jump!

Hemp's laughter is heard for the last time. The sound turns into a dying cry as the man plunges from the roof and hits the ground with a thump. **GEMMA** *follows his final trajectory.*

(reacting to this) Ugggh! Serve you right! You all right, Tommy?

TOMMY *(getting fainter)* Fine, love. You know me, bullet-proof, me.

GEMMA Can you manage to walk? Think you can make it as far as the car?

TOMMY Yes, fine. I'm fine, love...

ALGY But Tommy Middlebrass realised he was already a dying man.

GEMMA *(helping him, with difficulty)* Come on, then. Up you come. Lean on me! Lean on me, Tommy.

TOMMY *(wincing with pain)* Ah!

ALGY So this was how it felt to die, thought Tommy...

GEMMA *(as they make their way)* He could never shoot you, could he? You're Tommy Middlebrass, aren't you...?

TOMMY *(weakly)* I'm Tommy Middlebrass.

ALGY As his lifeblood oozed away, Tommy felt the darkness descending...

TOMMY *(faintly)* I'm Tommy Middlebrass.

GEMMA They can't kill Tommy Middlebrass – come on, guv, nearly there...

ALGY Gemma struggled to help the dying man back to the car...

GEMMA *(as they start to go off)* Easy does it, now. Just a few more steps. Easy, Tommy, easy now...

TOMMY *(feebly)* I'm Tommy Middlebrass... Tommy Middlebrass...

TOMMY, *supported by* **GEMMA**, *goes off.*

ALGY Gemma, with Peggy's help, gently eased Tommy into the passenger seat. His voice grew even fainter now, his breathing faster and shallower, as he repeated his name over and over again. Until his voice became little more than a whisper and finally he sat there silently, staring through sightless eyes at the windscreen. At last, gradually, inevitably, Death came to Tommy Middlebrass.

GEMMA *(off, a final, despairing cry of grief)* Tommy!

ALGY, *having finally done the deed, mirroring his hero, stares at his computer screen with sightless eyes.*

A respectful pause.

TOMMY *returns for a final outburst directed directly at* **ALGY**.

TOMMY *(shouting at* **ALGY***)* You can't kill me, I'm Tommy Middlebrass! I'm bloody immortal! I'll live a damn sight longer than you will, Waterbridge, you bastard!

He goes off again.

ALGY *sits, rather shaken.*

ALGY *(to himself)* Oh, my God, what have I done? What the hell have I done?

After a moment, **THELMA** *comes hurrying on. The lights return to their daylight state.*

THELMA *(excitedly)* Two million, seven hundred and seventy-four thousand, six hundred and sixty-two. And counting. That's still counting!

ALGY *(distractedly)* What?

THELMA Hits! On the website! Your website! Coming up to three million! Isn't that amazing? And they're still pouring in! Isn't it amazing? I believe it's what's known as going viral! *(noticing the state he is in)* Algy, what's the matter? What on earth's wrong?

ALGY *(shaking his head, dazed)* My God, I think I've just murdered someone!

As he sits there the lights fade to a:

Blackout.

Scene Two

The same. Mid-morning the following day.

*ALGY enters from the house, talking into the cordless
phone, listening to someone who is obviously in full flow.*

ALGY *(listening)* ...Yes...yes...yes... No, quite... Yes... He does,
he sounds a bit of a handful... Takes after his grandfather, I
think... Yes, well, you were at that age, too, I seem to recall...
A family trait, yes... Curse of the Waterbridges... Listen,
darling, it's so good of you to ring... Yes, well, I know it must
have been a bit of a shock for you... It was for me, I can tell
you... No, a pure misunderstanding... Idiot journalist... Too
complicated to go into now, yes... No, I'm perfectly fine,
promise... Got a few good years in me yet, with any luck...
Yes of course...nonetheless, I'm very touched you rang...
there was really no need to – yes, I know, I know I am, you
don't have to remind me... I just feel guilty I haven't been a
better one. Yes, yes, I know...all the same... Oh she's fine...
pretty good. Good days and bad days, you know...comes
and goes a bit... Yes, I realise, yes...progressive... Yes... Yes,
well we'll have to see... I feel she needs to be kept at home
as long as possible – she needs the reassurance, familiar
things around her, you know, things she recognises – even
if she's recognising less and less... Yes, it's going to cost,
there's going to be a cost, I want the best for her, the very
best... Yes, well, that's sweet of you both... I will... I'll let
you know if we need to call on you... Yes, promise... Yes...
And us to all of you, darling... Bye.

He stands for a moment, holding the phone.

He appears genuinely touched.

THELMA *enters from the house.*

That was nice of her. All the way from Canada. Must have
cost a bit.

THELMA You should try ringing her now and again.

ALGY We aren't that close, not these days.

THELMA When I answered just now, she sounded really concerned. I mean, all this business over that wretched obituary, even if it turned out to be a false alarm, it must have upset her. It probably brought it home to her, that – time was getting on. None of us was getting any younger. She only had you both for a while longer. I mean, we tend to take people for granted in a way, don't we? Our parents, our loved ones. When we're young we think they'll simply go on and on forever. I know I did with my father, he always seemed so full of life, so – immortal. Right up till the day he dropped dead in the garden, pruning the roses.

ALGY She's never seemed that fond of me. Seemed to prefer her mother, mostly. Always a bit distant with me.

THELMA Possibly you were a bit distant with her, maybe?

ALGY Possibly.

THELMA You and your relationships, Algy. Honestly. It defeats me how you can show such brilliant insight into your characters and yet in real life you can barely relate with anyone...

ALGY Because people in real life are generally irritating and unpredictable and ultimately disappointing. Unlike my characters who bloody well behave themselves and do as they're told. Most of them.

A slight pause.

Most of the time.

THELMA (*sorrowfully*) I don't know what we're going to do with you, I really don't.

She moves towards the house.

Oh, yes, I meant to tell you – your phone call put it right out of my mind – your publisher phoned earlier.

ALGY My ex-publisher, don't you mean? What did he want?

THELMA No, it wasn't Jason Ratcliffe, it was his assistant.

ALGY He only talks to his important clients, these days, I see...

THELMA He's probably terrified to talk to you. No, it was his assistant, Carlotta. She had some rather exciting news...

ALGY Exciting?

THELMA Well, she thought it was exciting and I thought it was exciting, too. I'm not sure whether you'll think it's exciting. Probably not, knowing you. But then you rarely find anything exciting these days, do you? But the exciting news is, with all this Internet interest in the website – it's currently up to four and a half million hits now, literally overnight – your publishers have had a preliminary enquiry from The Disney Company, expressing an interest in taking an option on the *Silly Milly* series...

ALGY *(incredulous)* Disney? And *Silly Milly*?

THELMA Yes. Doesn't that sound exciting?

ALGY It sounds positively ghastly. Can't think of anything worse. Disney? *Silly Milly*? No, out of the question. Tell them to get stuffed.

THELMA I just knew you'd say that! I knew it! I just knew you'd react like that, Algy. The moment someone comes along with an exciting idea –

ALGY I'm not having Disney buggering up my work! Resetting it all in Kansas, for Christ's sake!

THELMA They're not going to set it in Kansas...

ALGY Did you see that plasticised travesty they made of *Winnie the Pooh*? Little short of blasphemy. One of the great English classic children's books of all time and they go and stick a bloody gopher in the middle of it! A gopher, for Christ's sake? In Sussex? You could practically hear Alan Milne's ghost screaming from the Hundred Acre Wood. All those jarring American accents – "Oh, Pooh! Oh, gee, Piglet –"

THELMA *(impatiently)* Yes, all right, all right, Algy! You clearly don't think it's exciting. Carlotta thought it was exciting, I thought it was very, very exciting and I think most people would find it extremely exciting. You're apparently the only person in the world who doesn't find it exciting –

ALGY *(angrily)* And, in this case, I'm the only person in the world that matters! It's my work, my copyright and you can tell them to get stuffed from me!

THELMA Yes all right, all right! I'll – tell them – you're – intrigued by the idea. But – regretfully you're – too busy with other projects just at present to pursue it. I can't possibly tell The Disney Company to get stuffed, Algy, I can't!

ALGY Why not? Make Mickey Mouse's eyes water, anyway. I don't care, tell them what you like. Just get 'em off my back.

THELMA *goes out, sighing and shaking her head, taking the phone with her.*

ALGY *paces the garden, restlessly.*

He finally sits on the bench.

(in his Middlebrass voice) Aye, lass, there's been rough times in Grimthorpe, of late... *(a pause, sadly)* God, I miss the old bugger. I miss him already...

He sits sadly in the sunshine for a moment.

JESSICA *enters from the house. She is dressed rather formally and soberly, including hat and gloves.*

JESSICA Oh, hello, there.

ALGY Hello.

JESSICA Just taking a breather, are you?

ALGY Sorry?

JESSICA Taking a break from your labours? How are you getting on with it? Are you any nearer to finding that wretched blockage?

ALGY The –? No, Jess, I'm not the... *(giving up)* Oh, what the hell... *(assuming the persona of drainage expert, not a million miles from his Middlebrass)* Just about there, Madam. Couple more decent shoves, we'll have it all clear for you. Flowing like new. Like a mountain stream, love, it'll be.

JESSICA I must say, it's taken you long enough...

ALGY Bit of a tricky one this. Kinky pipes, you know. Aye, these old properties...

He sucks his teeth.

JESSICA Oh, yes, quite...

ALGY Beautiful, mind you, but most of them, they've got very kinky plumbing.

JESSICA Yes, I can imagine. We've lived here for ages, you know, ever since we moved from London. We wanted our daughter to be brought up in the country. We felt it would be a better life for her, you see. A much healthier lifestyle. And then my husband's work also – well, he wanted to move away, too. He found he wrote better in rural surroundings.

ALGY He would do, aye.

JESSICA Yes, on the whole, we've been very happy here.

She reflects for a moment.

(frowning) At least I think we have. *(pulling herself together)* Well, I can't sit around here gossiping. I must get on or else I'll be late.

She rises...

ALGY You're looking very smart, love. Don't mind me saying?

JESSICA *(a trifle surprised)* Me? Oh, all this...? Yes, it's rather sad really. It's a sad day for me, you see...

ALGY Yes?

JESSICA I'm shortly off to bury my husband.

ALGY Ah.

JESSICA It's his funeral today, you see...

ALGY Oh, I'm sorry to hear that, love...

JESSICA Yes, it's very sad. The saddest thing of all, of course, is I didn't even know he'd died –

ALGY Really?

JESSICA Nobody thought to tell me, you know...

ALGY That can't be right, can it...

JESSICA ...You'd have thought they could have at least let me know...

ALGY ...Least they could have done.

JESSICA ...Being his widow, I should surely have been the first one to be told, you'd have thought...

ALGY ...You'd have thought...

JESSICA ...As it was, I found out purely by accident. I happened to come across this old newspaper, Mrs. Henshaw was about to use it to wrap up some rubbish. And I saw my husband's obituary...

ALGY ...Must have come as a shock...

JESSICA ...A terrible shock. Mind you, it was very well-written... lovely sentiments. Mind you, it bore absolutely no resemblance to him, whatsoever, but then what can you expect from an obituary? They're mostly cosmetic, aren't they? Like the body they finally lay out in the coffin, all pink and smiling and looking as if butter wouldn't melt in its mouth. All the wrinkles and grumpy frown lines smoothed away. But he was a much more complex man than that, my husband. Much more complex. He wasn't a very pleasant man, you know, not when you first met him. Talk about having grumpy frown lines. He was covered in them. He didn't come over initially as being at all nice. You could hardly get a civilised hello out of the man, not on a first meeting. He was almost surly to me at first. But I persevered. I stuck at it. All my girlfriends said to me, "Jess, leave him, leave him alone, stand well clear, girl! The man's not worth it! He's really not worth the effort!" But, in the end, he was, you see. Well worth the effort. For me he was. As I slowly – unpicked him. Began to discover his inner workings. I found inside, such a kindness, such a caring, such an understanding. Such love. He gave me such love, you know. Mind you, you couldn't always see. He took great care to hide it from me, most of the time. Probably because it embarrassed him. Which was a great shame. For him. It's a wonderful feeling to receive love, of course, but it's so much more rewarding when you're actually giving it. All the same, I knew it was there. His love. All the time I knew it was there. And I loved him too. But, come to think of it, in the end, I was probably no better at showing it than he was.

A pause. They sit side-by-side on the bench in silence.

My greatest sadness, of course, is that he'll no longer be here to care for me.

ALGY Think you'll find he will be, love. For as long as you need him, any road.

JESSICA That's a sweet thought, thank you. I'm not sure whether I really believe all that sort of stuff, you know, loved ones looking down on us, but thank you for the thought, anyway.

ALGY *gently reaches out and touches her hand.* **JESSICA,** *aware of this, allows it to linger for a second.*

(after a pause) I say, shouldn't you be getting back to your drains?

ALGY Aye, yes. Of course. My drains.

JESSICA *(rising)* I must get along to the church now. Lovely to have talked to you. *(considering)* I think I need to go this way to get there, I think. Yes.

She moves towards the gate.

JESSICA See you later, if you're still here when I get back.

ALGY Yes, see you later. I hope my – I hope the funeral goes well.

JESSICA *(as she goes)* As long as they don't start singing hymns, that's all. He hated hymns, couldn't stand them.

ALGY *(under his breath)* He still can't...

JESSICA *goes off through the gate.*

ALGY *remains where he is.*

God. This is all getting somewhat surreal.

THELMA *comes out once more.*

THELMA *(as she enters)* Where on earth's she gone now? I saw you talking. Did she know who you were?

ALGY Not a clue. Thinks I'm the local drainage expert.

THELMA Oh, that's a shame. I had hoped she might have recognised you. She's dead set on going to this funeral of yours. If she'd only realised you were still alive that would have given her good reason not to have gone. I'd better try and catch her up and stop her.

ALGY What gave her the idea there was even a funeral today? Where'd she get that from?

THELMA She arranged it herself.

ALGY She did?

THELMA The minute she'd read that wretched obituary – I told Mrs. Henshaw to throw it away, to get rid of it – stupid woman. As soon as Jessica saw it, she promptly phoned the vicar and asked him when the funeral was. And, you know Michael Tipton, poor man, he was totally bemused because he hadn't the faintest idea you were even dead in the first place. Which of course you weren't. So Michael immediately phones me and I explained about the confusion and that I'd speak to Jessica to try and talk her out of it and he was not to worry. But then Jessica goes and phones him up again demanding to know exactly what day the funeral was going to be. And you know what Michael's like, he's well-meaning and woolly and he just panicked and he told Jessica it was today. And, when he told me, I said to him, what on earth was he going to do by way of a service? I mean, nobody was going to be there, were they, not a soul, apart from Jessica? And what's more, there was no one to bury. It's all turned into a complete nightmare. Well, I'm sorry but I certainly don't intend being there. I've far too much work to do without having to worry about your funeral.

ALGY I don't think she should be wandering down to the village on her own, sitting in an empty church, do you?

THELMA Well, can't you run after her to try and explain it?

ALGY She won't listen to me. I'm just the man from Dyno Rod.

THELMA *(turning to go)* No, all right I'll do it, I'll do it. She can't have gone far, not in her condition. *(as she starts to go)* Why is it always left to me? Everything's always left to me...

ALGY By the way, have you spoken to the publishers, yet? Have you called them back?

THELMA *(stopping)* What? No, not yet.

ALGY Only I think I may have changed my mind.

THELMA Changed your mind?

ALGY I think I'll give that Disney thing a shot, you know. After all, what have we got to lose, eh?

THELMA What's brought this about?

ALGY I just – had – a further think about it. We could do with the money, if nothing else.

THELMA You're quite certain? I mean, they're saying they want to commission a treatment. That doesn't mean they necessarily want to set it in Kansas but you may not care for their suggestions. And I really couldn't face months and months being stuck in the middle of terrible rows between Disney and Tommy Middlebrass, I simply couldn't face that.

ALGY He'll keep well on the sidelines, I promise.

THELMA *(suspiciously)* Really?

ALGY He's actually considering a new career.

THELMA *(puzzled)* Sorry?

ALGY If the worst comes to the worst, you can always tell them I'm dead.

THELMA Yes. Well. I think you've made the right decision, Algy, I really do. This could be the start of something really exciting, couldn't it? I must catch Jessica before she ends up in someone's garden, again...

She goes off through the gate.

ALGY *studies the garden, thoughtfully.*

ALGY *(to himself)* Hope I'm doing the right thing, anyway. Time will tell, I suppose...

JESSICA *enters from the house.*

JESSICA *(calling to him)* I say...

ALGY Oh, hello, you're there.

JESSICA I'm sorry I don't know your name?

ALGY What, mine? It's – Horace.

JESSICA Horace?

ALGY Yes.

JESSICA That's unusual.

ALGY Isn't it?

JESSICA You don't come across many Horaces these days, do you? Listen, Horace, if I can tear you away from your drains – it's just I'm off to the church, you see, for my husband's funeral...

ALGY Yes, so you told me...

JESSICA Only I can't find the church. I think it must have been relocated. It's so infuriating, they keep doing it all the time, these days, with everything.

ALGY Would you like me to – help you to look for it, love?

JESSICA If you would be so kind, thank you.

ALGY Can't be far away, can it?

JESSICA That is kind of you, thank you...

ALGY *(proffering his arm)* Here, love, would you like...?

JESSICA Oh, thank you. How gallant.

ALGY Oh, we drainage men, we know how to treat a lady...

They start walking arm-in-arm towards the back gate.

JESSICA *(as they go)* Now, I'm not sure quite who else is going to be there, exactly. You probably won't know a single soul...

ALGY I'll probably know one or two of them, love... Bound to.

As they both go off together, the lights fade to a:

Blackout.

End of Play

FURNITURE AND PROPS

Desk

Laptop and stand

Swivel chair at desk with cushion

Armchair

Side table

Bench

Slip of paper – email about Gus Crewes

Newspaper with obituary

Recorder

Small flip notebook and pen

House phone with hands-free handset

Tray

Two glasses of water

Prosecco bottle in freezer sleeve

Two champagne flutes filled with Prosecco

Wine glasses for pink tonic

Beer glasses

Two bunches of flowers

Jason's mobile phone

SOUND CUES

LIGHTING

ABOUT THE AUTHOR

Alan Ayckbourn has worked in theatre as a playwright and director for over fifty years, rarely if ever tempted by television or film, which perhaps explains why he continues to be so prolific. To date he has written more than eighty plays, many one-act plays and a large amount of work for the younger audience. His work has been translated into over thirty-five languages, is performed on stage and television throughout the world and has won countless awards.

Major successes include: *Relatively Speaking, How the Other Half Loves, Absurd Person Singular, Bedroom Farce, A Chorus of Disapproval*, and *The Norman Conquests*. In recent years, there have been revivals of *Season's Greetings* and *A Small Family Business* at the National Theatre; in the West End *Absent Friends, A Chorus of Disapproval, Relatively Speaking* and *How the Other Half Loves*; and at Chichester Festival Theatre, major revivals of *Way Upstream* in 2015 and *The Norman Conquests* in 2017. 2019 also saw the publication of his first work of prose fiction, *The Divide*.

Artistic director of the Stephen Joseph Theatre from 1972–2009, where almost all his plays have been first staged, he continues to direct his latest new work there. He was honoured to be appointed the SJT's first Director Emeritus during 2018. He has been inducted into the American Theater Hall of Fame, received the 2010 Critics' Circle Award for Services to the Arts and became the first British playwright to receive both Olivier and Tony Special Lifetime Achievement Awards. He was knighted in 1997 for services to the theatre.

Ten Times Table

Things We Do for Love

This Is Where We Came In

Time and Time Again

Time of My Life

Tons of Money (revised)

Way Upstream

Wildest Dreams

Wolf at the Door

Woman in Mind

A Word from Our Sponsor

**Other plays by ALAN AYCKBOURN
licensed by Concord Theatricals**

The Boy Who Fell Into a Book

Invisible Friends

The Jollies

Orvin – Champion of Champions

Surprises

Whenever

**FIND PERFECT PLAYS TO PERFORM AT
concordtheatricals.co.uk**